Edward Gibbon

A Vindication of Some Passages Etc.

Secon Edition

Edward Gibbon

A Vindication of Some Passages Etc.
Secon Edition

ISBN/EAN: 9783337812294

Printed in Europe, USA, Canada, Australia, Japan

Cover: Foto ©Thomas Meinert / pixelio.de

More available books at **www.hansebooks.com**

A VINDICATION

OF

SOME PASSAGES

IN THE

Fifteenth and Sixteenth Chapters

OF THE

HISTORY of the DECLINE and FALL of the ROMAN EMPIRE.

BY THE AUTHOR,

THE SECOND EDITION.

LONDON:

A

VINDICATION,

&c. &c.

PERHAPS it may be neceſſary to inform the Public, that not long ſince an Examination of the Fifteenth and Sixteenth Chapters of the Hiſtory of the Decline and Fall of the Roman Empire was publiſhed by Mr. Davis. He ſtyles himſelf a Bachelor of Arts, and a Member of Baliol College in the Univerſity of Oxford. His title-page is a declaration of war, and in the proſecution of his religious cruſade, he aſſumes a privilege of diſregarding the ordinary laws which are reſpected in the moſt hoſtile tranſactions between civilized men or civilized nations. Some of the harſheſt epithets in the Engliſh language are repeatedly applied to the hiſtorian, a part

of

of whofe work Mr. Davis has chofen for the object of his criticifm. To this author Mr. Davis imputes the crime of betraying the confidence and feducing the faith of thofe readers, who may heedlefsly ftray in the flowery paths of his diction, without perceiving the poifonous fnake that lurks concealed in the grafs. *Latet anguis in herbâ.* The Examiner has affumed the province of reminding them of "the unfair "proceedings of fuch an infidious friend, who "offers the deadly draught in a golden cup, "that they may be lefs fenfible of the danger[1]. "In order to which, Mr. Davis has felected "feveral of the more notorious inftances of his "mifreprefentations and errors; reducing them "to their refpective heads, and fubjoining a "long lift of almoft incredible inaccuracies: "and fuch ftriking proofs of fervile plagiarifm, "as the world will be furprifed to meet with "in an author who puts in fo bold a claim to "originality and extenfive reading[2]?" Mr. Davis profecutes this attack through an octavo volume of not lefs than two hundred and eighty-four pages with the fame implacable fpirit; perpetually charges his adverfary with perverting the ancients, and tranfcribing the moderns; and, inconfiftently enough, imputes to him the oppofite crimes of art and careleffnefs, of grofs

[1] Davis, Preface, p. ii. [2] Ibid. Preface, p. iii.

ignorance and of wilful falsehood. The Examiner closes his work [3] with a severe reproof of those feeble critics who have allowed any share of knowledge to an odious antagonist. He presumes to pity and to condemn the first historian of the present age, for the generous approbation which he had bestowed on a writer who is content that Mr. Davis should be his enemy, whilst he has a right to name Dr. Robertson for his friend.

When I delivered to the world the First Volume of an important History, in which I had been obliged to connect the progress of Christianity with the civil state and revolutions of the Roman Empire, I could not be ignorant that the result of my inquiries might offend the interest of some and the opinions of others. If the whole work was favourably received by the Public, I had the more reason to expect that this obnoxious part would provoke the zeal of those who consider themselves as the Watchmen of the Holy City. These expectations were not disappointed; and a fruitful crop of Answers, Apologies, Remarks, Examinations, &c. sprung up with all convenient speed. As soon as I saw the advertisement, I generally sent for them; for I have never affected, indeed I have never understood, the

[3] Davis, p. 282, 283.

ſtoical apathy, the proud contempt of criticiſm, which ſome authors have publicly profeſſed. Fame is the motive, it is the reward, of our labours; nor can I eaſily comprehend how it is poſſible that we ſhould remain cold and indifferent with regard to the attempts which are made to deprive us of the moſt valuable object of our poſſeſſions, or at leaſt of our hopes. Beſides this ſtrong and natural impulſe of curioſity, I was prompted by the more laudable deſire of applying to my own, and the public, benefit, the well-grounded cenſures of a learned adverſary; and of correcting thoſe faults which the indulgence of vanity and friendſhip had ſuffered to eſcape without obſervation. I read with attention ſeveral criticiſms which were publiſhed againſt the Two laſt Chapters of my Hiſtory, and unleſs I much deceive myſelf, I weighed them in my own mind without prejudice and without reſentment. After I was clearly ſatisfied that their principal objections were founded on miſrepreſentation or miſtake, I declined with ſincere and diſintereſted reluctance the odious taſk of controverſy, and almoſt formed a tacit reſolution of committing my intentions, my writings, and my adverſaries to the judgment of the Public, of whoſe favourable diſpoſition I had received the moſt flattering proofs.

The

The reasons which justified my silence were obvious and forcible: the respectable nature of the subject itself, which ought not to be rashly violated by the rude hand of controversy; the inevitable tendency of dispute, which soon degenerates into minute and personal altercation; the indifference of the Public for the discussion of such questions as neither relate to the business nor the amusement of the present age. I calculated the possible loss of temper and the certain loss of time, and considered, that while I was laboriously engaged in a humiliating task, which could add nothing to my own reputation, or to the entertainment of my readers, I must interrupt the prosecution of a work which claimed my whole attention, and which the Public, or at least my friends, seemed to require with some impatience at my hands. The judicious lines of Dr. Young sometimes offered themselves to my memory, and I felt the truth of his observation, That every author lives or dies by his own pen, and that the unerring sentence of Time assigns its proper rank to every composition and to every criticism, which it preserves from oblivion.

I should have consulted my own ease, and perhaps I should have acted in stricter conformity to the rules of prudence, if I had still persevered in patient silence. But Mr. Davis may, if he pleases, assume the merit of extort-

ing

ing from me the notice which I had refuſed to more honourable foes. I had declined the conſideration of their *literary Objections*; but he has compelled me to give an anſwer to his *criminal Accuſations*. Had he confined himſelf to the ordinary, and indeed obſolete charges of impious principles, and miſchievous intentions, I ſhould have acknowledged with readineſs and pleaſure that the religion of Mr. Davis appeared to be very different from mine. Had he contented himſelf with the uſe of that ſtyle which decency and politeneſs have baniſhed from the more liberal part of mankind, I ſhould have ſmiled, perhaps with ſome contempt, but without the leaſt mixture of anger or reſentment. Every animal employs the note, or cry, or howl, which is peculiar to its ſpecies; every man expreſſes himſelf in the dialect the moſt congenial to his temper and inclination, the moſt familiar to the company in which he has lived, and to the authors with whom he is converſant; and while I was diſpoſed to allow that Mr. Davis had made ſome proficiency in Eccleſiaſtical Studies, I ſhould have conſidered the difference of our language and manners as an unſurmountable bar of ſeparation between us. Mr. Davis has overleaped that bar, and forces me to contend with him on the very dirty ground which he has choſen for the ſcene of

our

our combat. He has judged, I know not with how much propriety, that the ſupport of a cauſe, which would diſclaim ſuch unworthy aſſiſtance, depended on the ruin of my moral and literary character. The different miſrepreſentations, of which he has drawn out the ignominious catalogue, would materially affect my credit as an hiſtorian, my reputation as a ſcholar, and even my honour and veracity as a gentleman. If I am indeed incapable of underſtanding what I read, I can no longer claim a place among thoſe writers who merit the eſteem and confidence of the Public. If I am capable of wilfully perverting what I underſtand, I no longer deſerve to live in the ſociety of thoſe men, who conſider a ſtrict and inviolable adherence to truth, as the foundation of every thing that is virtuous or honourable in human nature. At the ſame time, I am not inſenſible that his mode of attack has given a tranſient pleaſure to my enemies, and a tranſient uneaſineſs to my friends. The ſize of his volume, the boldneſs of his aſſertions, the acrimony of his ſtyle, are contrived with tolerable ſkill to confound the ignorance and candour of his readers. There are few who will examine the truth or juſtice of his accuſations; and of thoſe perſons who have been directed by their education to the ſtudy of eccleſiaſtical antiquity,

many

many will believe, or will affect to believe, that the succefs of their champion has been equal to his zeal, and that the *ferpent* pierced with an hundred wounds lies expiring at his feet. Mr. Davis's book *will* ceafe to be read (perhaps the grammarians may already reproach me for the ufe of an improper tenfe); but the oblivion towards which it feems to be haftening, will afford the more ample fcope for the artful practices of thofe, who may not fcruple to affirm, or rather to infinuate, that Mr. Gibbon was publickly convicted of falfehood and mifreprefentation; that the evidence produced againft him was unanfwerable; and that his filence was the effect and the proof of confcious guilt. Under the hands of a malicious furgeon, the fting of a wafp may continue to fefter and inflame, long after the vexatious little infect has left its venom and its life in the wound.

The defence of my own honour is undoubtedly the firft and prevailing motive which urges me to repel with vigour an unjuft and unprovoked attack; and to undertake a tedious vindication, which, after the perpetual repetition of the vaineft and moft difgufting of the pronouns, will only prove that *I* am innocent; and that Mr. Davis, in his charge, has very frequently fubfcribed his own condemnation. And yet I may preſume to affirm, that the Public have ſome intereſt in this controverſy. They have ſome intereſt to know, whether the writer whom they have honoured with their favour is deſerving of their confidence, whether they muſt content themſelves with reading the Hiſtory of the Decline and Fall of the Roman Empire as a *tale amuſing enough*, or whether they may venture to receive it as a fair and authentic hiſtory. The general perſuaſion of mankind, that where *much* has been poſitively aſſerted, *ſomething* muſt be true, may contribute to encourage a ſecret ſuſpicion, which would naturally diffuſe itſelf over the whole body of the work. Some of thoſe friends who may now tax me with imprudence for taking this public notice of Mr. Davis's book, have perhaps already condemned me for ſilently acquieſcing under the weight of ſuch ſerious, ſuch direct, and ſuch circumſtantial imputations.

Mr. Davis, who in the laſt page of his [4] Work appears to have recollected that modeſty is an amiable and uſeful qualification, affirms, that his plan required only that he ſhould conſult the authors to whom he was directed by my references; and that the judgment of riper

[4] Davis, p. 284.

years was not ſo neceſſary to enable him to execute with ſucceſs the pious labour to which he had devoted his pen. Perhaps, before we ſeparate, a moment to which I moſt fervently aſpire, Mr. Davis may find that a mature judgment is indiſpenſably requiſite for the ſucceſsful execution of *any* work of literature, and more eſpecially of criticiſm. Perhaps he will diſcover, that a young ſtudent, who haſtily conſults an unknown author, on a ſubject with which he is unacquainted, cannot always be guided by the moſt accurate reference to the knowledge of the ſenſe, as well as to the ſight of the paſſage which has been quoted by his adverſary. Abundant proofs of theſe maxims will hereafter be ſuggeſted. For the preſent, I ſhall only remark, that it is my intention to purſue in my defence the order, or rather the courſe, which Mr. Davis has marked out in his Examination; and that I have numbered the ſeveral articles of my impeachment according to the moſt natural diviſion of the ſubject. And now let me proceed on this hoſtile march over a dreary and barren deſert, where thirſt, hunger, and intolerable wearineſs, are much more to be dreaded, than the arrows of the enemy.

I. " The

I.

"The remarkable mode of quotation which "Mr. Gibbon adopts, must immediately strike "every one who turns to his notes. He some- "times only mentions the author, perhaps the "book; and often leaves the reader the toil "of finding out, or rather guessing at the pas- "sage. The policy, however, is not without "its design and use. By endeavouring to de- "prive us of the means of comparing him with "the authorities he cites, he flattered himself, "no doubt, that he might safely have recourse "to *misrepresentation*[5]." Such is the style of Mr. Davis; who in another place[6] mentions this mode of quotation "as a good artifice to "escape detection;" and applauds, with an agreeable irony, his own labours in turning over a *few* pages of the Theodosian Code.

QUOTATIONS IN GENERAL.

I shall not descend to animadvert on the rude and illiberal strain of this passage, and I will frankly own that my indignation is lost in astonishment. The Fifteenth and Sixteenth Chapters of my History are illustrated by three hundred and eighty-three Notes; and the nakedness of a few Notes, which are not accompanied by any quotation, is amply compensated by a much greater number, which contain two, three, or perhaps four distinct

[5] Davis, Preface, p. ii.

[6] Id. p. 230.

references; so that upon the whole my stock of quotations which support and justify my facts cannot amount to less than eight hundred or a thousand. As I had often felt the inconvenience of the loose and general method of quoting which is so falsely imputed to me, I have carefully distinguished the *books*, the *chapters*, the *sections*, the *pages* of the authors to whom I referred, with a degree of accuracy and attention, which might claim some gratitude, as it has seldom been so regularly practised by any historical writers. And here I must confess some obligation to Mr. Davis, who, by staking my credit and his own on a circumstance so obvious and palpable, has given me this early opportunity of submitting the merits of our cause, or at least of our characters, to the judgment of the Public. Hereafter, when I am summoned to defend myself against the imputation of misquoting the text, or misrepresenting the sense of a Greek or Latin author, it will not be in my power to communicate the knowledge of the languages, or the possession of the books, to those readers who may be destitute either of one or of the other, and the part which *they* are obliged to take between assertions equally strong and peremptory, may sometimes be attended with doubt and hesitation. But, in the present in-

stance,

ſtance, every reader who will give himſelf the trouble of conſulting the Firſt Volume of my Hiſtory, is a competent judge of the queſtion. I exhort, I ſolicit him to run his eye down the columns of Notes, and to count *how many* of the quotations are minute and particular, *how few* are vague and general. When he has ſatisfied himſelf by this eaſy computation, there *is* a word which may naturally ſuggeſt itſelf; an epithet, which I ſhould be ſorry either to deſerve or uſe; the boldneſs of Mr. Davis's aſſertion, and the confidence of my appeal, will tempt, nay, perhaps, will force him to apply that epithet either to one or to the other of the adverſe parties.

I have confeſſed that a critical eye may diſcover *ſome* looſe and general references; but as they bear a very *inconſiderable* proportion to the whole maſs, they cannot ſupport, or even excuſe, a falſe and ungenerous accuſation, which muſt reflect diſhonour either on the object or on the author of it. If the examples in which I have occaſionally deviated from my ordinary practice were ſpecified and examined, I am perſuaded that they might always be fairly attributed to one of the following reaſons. 1. In ſome *rare* inſtances, which I have never attempted to conceal, I have been obliged to adopt quotations which were expreſſed with leſs accuracy than I could have wiſhed. 2. I may have accidentally recollected the ſenſe of a paſſage which I had formerly read, without being able to find the place, or even to tranſcribe from memory the preciſe words. 3. The whole tract (as in a remarkable inſtance of the ſecond Apology of Juſtin Martyr) was ſo ſhort, that a more particular deſcription was not required. 4. The form of the compoſition ſupplied the want of a local reference; the preceding mention of the *year* fixed the paſſage of the annaliſt; and the reader was guided to the proper ſpot in the commentaries of Grotius, Valeſius, or Godefroy, by the more accurate citation of their original author. 5. The idea which I was deſirous of communicating to the reader, was ſometimes the general reſult of the author or treatiſe that I had quoted; nor was it poſſible to confine, within the narrow limits of a particular reference, the ſenſe or ſpirit which was mingled with the whole maſs. Theſe motives are either laudable, or at leaſt innocent. In two of theſe exceptions, my ordinary mode of citation was ſuperfluous; in the other three, it was impracticable.

In quoting a compariſon which Tertullian had uſed to expreſs the rapid increaſe of the Marcionites, I expreſsly declared that I was obliged to quote it from memory [7]. If I have been guilty of comparing them to *bees* inſtead of *waſps*, I can however moſt ſincerely diſclaim

[7] Gibbon's Hiſtory, p. 551. I ſhall uſually refer to the third edition, unleſs there are any various readings.

the

the ſagacious ſuſpicion of Mr. Davis[8], who imagines that I was tempted to amend the ſimile of Tertullian from an improper partiality for thoſe odious Heretics.

A reſcript of Diocletian, which declared *the* old law (not *an* old law[9]), had been alleged by me on the reſpectable authority of Fra-Paolo. The Examiner, who thinks that he has turned over the pages of the Theodoſian Code, informs[1] his reader that it may be found, l. vi. tit. xxiv. leg. 8.; he will be ſurpriſed to learn that this reſcript could not be *found* in a code where it does not exiſt, but that it may diſtinctly be read in the ſame number, the ſame title, and the ſame book of the CODE OF JUSTINIAN. He who is ſevere ſhould at leaſt be juſt: yet I ſhould probably have diſdained this minute animadverſion, unleſs it had ſerved to diſplay the general ignorance of the critic in the Hiſtory of the Roman Juriſprudence. If Mr. Davis had not been an abſolute ſtranger, the moſt treacherous guide could not have perſuaded him that a reſcript of Diocletian was to be found in the Theodoſian Code, which was deſigned only to preſerve the laws of Conſtantine and his ſucceſſors. Compendioſam (ſays Theodoſius himſelf) Divalium Conſtitutionum ſcientiam, ex D. Conſtantini temporibus roboramus. (Novell. ad calcem Cod. Theod. l. i. tit. i. leg. 1.)

[8] Davis, p. 144. [9] Gibbon, p. 593. [1] Davis, p. 230.

II. Few

II.

ERRORS OF THE PRESS.

Few objects are below the notice of Mr. Davis, and his criticism is never so formidable as when it is directed against the guilty corrector of the press, who on some occasions has shewn himself negligent of my fame and of his own. Some errors have arisen from the omission of letters; from the confusion of cyphers, which perhaps were not very distinctly marked in the original manuscript. The *two* of the Roman, and the *eleven* of the Arabic, numerals have been unfortunately mistaken for each other; the similar forms of a 2 and a 3, a 5 and a 6, a 3 and an 8, have improperly been transposed; A*n*tolycus for A*u*tolycus, Idolatria for Ido*lo*latria, Holste*ri*us for Holste*n*ius, had escaped my own observation, as well as the diligence of the person who was employed to revise the sheets of my History. These important errors, from the indulgence of a deluded Public, have been multiplied in the numerous impressions of three different editions; and for the present I can only lament my own defects, whilst I deprecate the wrath of Mr. Davis, who seems ready to infer that I cannot either read or write. I sincerely admire his patient industry, which I despair of being able to imitate; but if a future edition should ever be required, I could wish to obtain, on any reasonable terms, the services of so useful a corrector.

III. Mr.

III.

Difference of Editions.

Mr. Davis had been directed by my references to several passages of Optatus Milevitanus [2], and of the Bibliotheque Ecclesiastique of M. Dupin [3]. He eagerly consults those places, is unsuccessful, and is happy. Sometimes the place which I have quoted does not offer any of the circumstances which I had alleged, sometimes only a few; and sometimes the same passages exhibit a sense totally adverse and repugnant to mine. These shameful misrepresentations incline Mr. Davis to suspect that I have never consulted the original (not even of a common French book!), and he asserts his right to censure my presumption. These important charges form two distinct articles in the list of *Misrepresentations*; but Mr. Davis has amused himself with adding to the slips of the pen or of the press, some complaints of his ill success, when he attempted to verify my quotations from Cyprian and from Shaw's Travels [4].

The success of Mr. Davis would indeed have been somewhat extraordinary, unless he had consulted the same *editions*, as well as the same places. I shall content myself with mention-

[2] Davis, p. 73. [3] Id. p. 132—136. [4] Id. p. 151. 155.

ing the editions which I have uſed, and with aſſuring him, that if he renews his ſearch, he will not, or rather that he will, be diſappointed.

Mr. Gibbon's Editions.	Mr. Davis's Editions.
Optatus Milevitanus, by Dupin, fol. Paris, 1700.	Fol. Antwerp, 1702.
Dupin, Bibliotheque Eccleſiaſtique, 4to. Paris, 1690.	8vo. Paris, 1687.
Cypriani Opera, Edit. Fell, fol. Amſterdam, 1700.	Moſt probably Oxon. 1682.
Shaw's Travels, 4to. London, 1757.	The folio Edition.

IV.

JEWISH HISTORY, TACITUS.

The nature of my ſubject had led me to mention, not the real origin of the Jews, but their firſt *appearance* to the eyes of other nations; and I cannot avoid tranſcribing the ſhort paſſage in which I had introduced them. "The Jews, who under the Aſſyrian and Perſian monarchies had languiſhed for many "ages the moſt deſpiſed portion of their "ſlaves, emerged from their obſcurity under "the ſucceſſors of Alexander. And as they "multiplied to a ſurpriſing degree in the Eaſt, "and afterwards in the Weſt, they ſoon excited the curioſity and wonder of other nations[5]." This ſimple abridgment ſeems in its turn to have excited the wonder of Mr. Davis, whoſe ſurpriſe almoſt renders him eloquent.

[5] Gibbon, p. 537.

"What

"What a strange assemblage," says he, "is
"here? It is like Milton's Chaos, without
"bound, without dimension, where time and
"place are lost. In short, what does this dis-
"play afford us, but a deal of boyish co-
"louring to the prejudice of much good his-
"tory[6]?" If I rightly understand Mr. Davis's language, he censures, as a piece of confused declamation, the passage which he has produced from my History; and if I collect the angry criticisms which he has scattered over twenty pages of controversy[7], I think I can discover that there is hardly a period, or even a word, in this unfortunate passage, which has obtained the approbation of the Examiner.

As nothing can escape his vigilance, he censures me for including the twelve tribes of Israel under the common appellation of JEWS[8], and for extending the name of ASSYRIANS to the subjects of the Kings of Babylon[9]; and again censures me, because some facts which are affirmed or insinuated in my text, do not agree with the strict and proper limits which he has assigned to those national denominations. The name of *Jews* has indeed been established by the scepter of the tribe of *Judah*, and, in the times which precede the captivity, it is used in the more

[6] Davis, p. 5. [7] Id. p. 2--22. [8] Id. p. 3. [9] Id. p. 2.

 general

general ſenſe with ſome ſort of impropriety; but ſurely I am not peculiarly charged with a fault which has been conſecrated by the conſent of twenty centuries, the practice of the beſt writers, ancient as well as modern (See Joſephus and Prideaux, even in the titles of their reſpective works), and by the uſage of modern languages, of the Latin, the Greek, and, if I may credit Reland, of the Hebrew itſelf (See Paleſtin. l. i. c. 6.). With regard to the other word, that of Aſſyrians, moſt aſſuredly I will not loſe myſelf in the labyrinth of the Aſiatic monarchies before the age of Cyrus; nor indeed is any more required for my juſtification, than to prove that Babylon was conſidered as the capital and royal ſeat of Aſſyria. If Mr. Davis were a man of learning, I might be moroſe enough to cenſure his ignorance of ancient geography, and to overwhelm him under a load of quotations, which might be collected and tranſcribed with very little trouble: But as I *muſt* ſuppoſe that he has received a claſſical education, I might have expected him to have read the firſt book of Herodotus, where that hiſtorian deſcribes, in the cleareſt and moſt elegant terms, the ſituation and greatneſs of Babylon: Της δε Ασσυριης τα μεν κου και αλλα πολισματα μεγαλα πολλα, το δε ονομαστοτατον και ισχυροτατον και ενθα σφι,

Νινου

Νινου αναστατου γενομενης, τα βασιληια κατιστηκει, τη Βαβυλων. (Clio, c. 178.) I may be ſurpriſed that he ſhould be ſo little converſant with the Cyropœdia of Xenophon, in the whole courſe of which the King of Babylon, the adverſary of the Medes and Perſians, is repeatedly mentioned by the ſtyle and title of THE ASSYRIAN, Ὁ δε Ασσυριος, ὁ Βαβυλωνα τε εχων και την αλλην Ασσυριαν. (l. ii. p. 102, 103, Edit. Hutchinſon.) But there remains ſomething more: and Mr. Davis muſt apply the ſame reproaches of *inaccuracy, if not ignorance*, to the Prophet Iſaiah, who, in the name of Jehovah, announcing the downfal of Babylon and the deliverance of Iſrael, declares with an oath; "And as I have pur-"poſed the thing ſhall ſtand: to cruſh the "ASSYRIAN in my land, and to trample him "on my mountains. Then ſhall his yoke de-"part from off them; and his burthen ſhall "be removed from off their ſhoulders." (Iſaiah, xiv. 24, 25. Lowth's new tranſlation. See likewiſe the Biſhop's note, p. 98.) Our old tranſlation expreſſes, with leſs elegance, the the ſame meaning; but I mention with pleaſure the labours of a reſpectable Prelate, who in this, as well as in a former work, has very happily united the moſt critical judgment, with the taſte and ſpirit of poetry.

The

The jealousy which Mr. Davis affects for the honour of the Jewish people, will not suffer him to allow that they were *slaves* to the conquerors of the East; and while he acknowledges that they were tributary and dependent, he seems desirous of introducing, or even inventing, some milder expression of the state of vassalage and *subservience* [1]; from whence Tacitus assumed the words of *despectissima pars servientium*. Has Mr. Davis never heard of the distinction of civil and political slavery? Is he ignorant that even the natural and victorious subjects of an Asiatic despot have been deservedly marked with the opprobrious epithet of slaves by every writer acquainted with the name and advantage of freedom? Does he not know that, under such a government, the yoke is imposed with double weight on the necks of the vanquished, as the rigour of tyranny is aggravated by the abuse of conquest. From the first invasion of Judæa by the arms of the Assyrians, to the subversion of the Persian monarchy by Alexander, there elapsed a period of above four hundred years, which included about twelve ages or generations of the human race. As long as the Jews asserted their independence, they repeatedly suffered every calamity which the rage and insolence of a vic-

[1] Davis, p. 6.

torious

torious enemy could inflict; the throne of David was overturned, the temple and city were reduced to ashes, and the whole land, a circumstance perhaps unparalleled in history, remained three-score and ten years without inhabitants, and without cultivation. (2 Chronicles, xxxvi. 21.) According to an institution which has long prevailed in Asia, and particularly in the Turkish government, the most beautiful and ingenious youths were carefully educated in the palace, where superior merit sometimes introduced these fortunate *slaves* to the favour of the conqueror, and to the honours of the state. (See the book and example of Daniel.) The rest of the unhappy Jews experienced the hardships of captivity and exile in distant lands, and while individuals were oppressed, the nation seemed to be dissolved or annihilated. The gracious edict of Cyrus was offered to all those who worshipped the God of Israel in the temple of Jerusalem; but it was accepted by no more than forty-two thousand persons of either sex and of every age, and of these about thirty thousand derived their origin from the Tribes of Judah, of Benjamin, and of Levi. (See Ezra, i. Nehemiah, vii. and Prideaux's Connections, vol. i. p. 107. fol. Edit. London, 1718.) The inconsiderable band of exiles, who returned to inhabit the land of their fathers, cannot be

x computed

computed as the hundred and fiftieth part of the mighty people that had been numbered by the impious raſhneſs of David. After a ſurvey, which did not comprehend the Tribes of Levi and Benjamin, the monarch was aſſured that he reigned over *one million five hundred and ſeventy thouſand men* that drew ſword (1 Chronicles, xxi. 1—6), and the country of Judæa muſt have contained near ſeven millions of free inhabitants. The progreſs of reſtoration is always leſs rapid than that of deſtruction; Jeruſalem, which had been ruined in a few months, was rebuilt by the ſlow and interrupted labours of a whole century; and the Jews, who gradually multiplied in their native ſeats, enjoyed a ſervile and precarious exiſtence, which depended on the capricious will of their maſter. The books of Ezra and Nehemiah do not afford a very pleaſing view of their ſituation under the Perſian Empire; and the book of Eſther exhibits a moſt extraordinary inſtance of the degree of eſtimation in which they were held at the Court of Suſa. A Miniſter addreſſed his King in the following words, which may be conſidered as a Commentary on the *deſpectiſſima pars ſervientium* of the Roman hiſtorian: "And Haman ſaid to "King Ahaſuerus, There is a certain people "ſcattered abroad, and diſperſed among the "people

"people in all the provinces of thy kingdom; "and their laws are diverse from all people, "neither keep they the King's laws; therefore "it is not for the King's profit to suffer them. "If it please the King, let it be written that "they may be destroyed; and I will pay ten "thousand talents of silver to the hands of "those that have the charge of the business, to "bring it to the King's treasuries. And the "king took his ring from his hand, and gave "it to Haman, the son of Hammedatha the "Agagite, the Jews' enemy. And the king "said unto Haman, The silver is given unto "thee; the people also, to do with them as "it seemeth good to thee." (Esther, iii. 8—11.) This trifling favour was asked by the Minister, and granted by the Monarch, with an easy indifference, which expressed their contempt for the lives and fortunes of the Jews; the business passed without difficulty through the forms of office; and had Esther been less lovely, or less beloved, a single day would have consummated the universal slaughter of a submissive people, to whom no legal defence was allowed, and from whom no resistance seems to have been dreaded. I am a stranger to Mr. Davis's political principles; but I should think that the epithet of *slaves*, and of *despised* slaves, may, without injustice, be applied to a captive nation, over whoſe head the ſword of tyranny was ſuſpended by ſo ſlender a thread.

The policy of the Macedonians was very different from that of the Perſians; and yet Mr. Davis, who reluctantly confeſſes that the Jews were oppreſſed by the former, does not underſtand how long they were favoured and protected by the latter[1]. In the ſhock of thoſe revolutions which divided the empire of Alexander, Judæa, like the other provinces, experienced the tranſient ravages of an advancing or retreating enemy, who led away a multitude of captives. But, in the age of Joſephus, the Jews ſtill enjoyed the privileges granted by the Kings of Aſia and Egypt, who had fixed numerous colonies of that nation in the new cities of Alexandria, Antioch, &c. and placed them in the ſame honourable condition (ισοπολιτας, ισοτιμας) as the Greeks and Macedonians themſelves. (Joſeph. Antiquitat. l. xii. c. 1. 3. p. 585. 596. Vol. i. edit. Havercamp.) Had they been treated with leſs indulgence, their ſettlement in thoſe celebrated cities, the ſeats of commerce and learning, was enough to introduce them to the knowledge of the world, and to juſtify my *abſurd* propoſition, that they emerged from obſcurity under the ſucceſſors of Alexander.

[1] Davis, p. 4.

The

The Jews remained and flouriſhed under the mild dominion of the Macedonian Princes, till they were compelled to aſſert their civil and religious rights againſt Antiochus Epiphanes, who had adopted new maxims of tyranny; and the age of the Maccabees is perhaps the moſt glorious period of the Hebrew annals. Mr. Davis, who on this occaſion is bewildered by the ſubtlety of Tacitus, does not comprehend why the hiſtorian ſhould aſcribe the independence of the Jews to three *negative* cauſes, "Macedonibus invalidis, Parthis nondum adultis, "et Romani procul aberant." To the underſtanding of the critic, Tacitus might as well have obſerved, that the Jews were not deſtroyed by a plague, a famine, or an earthquake; and Mr. Davis cannot ſee, for his own part, any reaſon why they might not have elected Kings of their own two or three hundred years before[3]. Such indeed was not the reaſon of Tacitus: he probably conſidered that every nation, depreſſed by the weight of a foreign power, naturally riſes towards the ſurface, as ſoon as the preſſure is removed; and he might think that, in a ſhort and rapid hiſtory of the independence of the Jews, it was ſufficient for him to ſhew that the obſtacles did not exiſt, which, in an earlier or in a later period,

[3] Davis, p. 8.

would have checked their efforts. The curious reader, who has leisure to study the Jewish and Syrian history, will discover, that the throne of the Asmonæan Princes was confirmed by the two great victories of the Parthians over Demetrius Nicator, and Antiochus Sidetes (See Joseph. Antiquitat. Jud. l. xiji. c. 5, 6. 8, 9. Justin, xxxvi. 1. xxxviii. 10. with Usher and Prideaux, before Christ 141 and 130); and the expression of Tacitus, the more closely it is examined, will be the more rationally admired.

My Quotations[4] are the object of Mr. Davis's criticism[5], as well as the Text of this short, but obnoxious passage. He corrects the error of my memory, which had suggested *servitutis* instead of *servientium*; and so natural is the alliance between truth and moderation, that on this occasion he forgets his character, and candidly acquits me of any malicious design to misrepresent the words of Tacitus. The other references, which are contained in the first and second Notes of my Fifteenth Chapter, are connected with each other, and can only be mistaken after they have been forcibly separated. The silence of Herodotus is a fair evidence of the obscurity of the Jews, who had escaped the eyes of so curious a traveller. The Jews are first mentioned by Justin, when he

[4] Gibbon, p. 537. Note 1, 2. [5] Davis, p. 10, 11. 20.

relates the siege of Jerusalem by Antiochus Sidetes; and the conquest of Judæa, by the arms of Pompey, engaged Diodorus and Dion to introduce that singular nation to the acquaintance of their readers. These epochs, which are within seventy years of each other, mark the age in which the Jewish people, emerging from their obscurity, began to act a part in the society of nations, and to excite the curiosity of the Greek and Roman historians. For that purpose only, I had appealed to the authority of Diodorus Siculus, of Justin, or rather of Trogus Pompeius, and of Dion Cassius. If I had designed to investigate the Jewish Antiquities, reason, as well as faith, must have directed my inquiries to the Sacred Books, which, even as human productions, would deserve to be studied as one of the most curious and original monuments of the East.

I stand accused, though not indeed by Mr. Davis, for profanely depreciating the *promised* Land, as well as the *chosen* People. The Gentleman without a name has placed this charge in the front of his battle[1], and if my memory does not deceive me, it is one of the few remarks in Mr. Apthorpe's book, which have any immediate relation to my History. They

[1] Remarks, p. 1.

seem

ſeem to conſider in the light of a reproach, and of an unjuſt reproach, the idea which I had given of Paleſtine, as of a territory ſcarcely ſuperior to Wales in extent and fertility [2]; and they ſtrangely convert a geographical obſervation into a theological error. When I recollect that the imputation of a ſimilar error was employed by the implacable Calvin, to precipitate and to juſtify the execution of Servetus, I muſt applaud the felicity of this country, and of this age, which has diſarmed, if it could not mollify, the fierceneſs of eccleſiaſtical criticiſm (See Dictionaire Critique de Chauffepié, tom. iv. p. 223).

As I had compared the narrow extent of Phœnicia and Paleſtine with the important bleſſings which thoſe celebrated countries had diffuſed over the reſt of the earth, their minute ſize became an object not of cenſure but of praiſe.

Ingentes animos anguſto in pectore verſant.

The preciſe meaſure of Paleſtine was taken from Templeman's Survey of the Globe: he allows to Wales 7011 ſquare Engliſh miles, to the Morea, or Peloponneſus, 7220, to the Seven United Provinces 7546, and to Judæa or Paleſtine 7600. The difference is not very conſiderable, and if any of theſe countries has

[2] Gibbon, p. 30.

been

been magnified beyond its real ſize, Aſia is more liable than Europe to have been affected by the inaccuracy of Mr. Templeman's maps. To the authority of this modern ſurvey, I ſhall only add the ancient and weighty teſtimony of Jerom, who paſſed in Paleſtine above thirty years of his life: From Dan to Berſhebah, the two fixed and proverbial boundaries of the Holy Land, he reckons no more than one hundred and ſixty miles (Hieronym. ad Dardanum, tom. iii. p. 66), and the breadth of Paleſtine cannot by any expedient be ſtretched to one half of its length (See Reland, Paleſtin. l. ii. c. 5. p. 421).

The degrees and limits of fertility cannot be aſcertained with the ſtrict ſimplicity of geographical meaſures. Whenever we ſpeak of the productions of the earth, in different climates, our ideas muſt be relative, our expreſſions vague and doubtful; nor can we always diſtinguiſh between the gifts of Nature and the rewards of Induſtry. The Emperor Frederick II., the enemy and the victim of the Clergy, is accuſed of ſaying, after his return from his Cruſade, that the God of the Jews would have deſpiſed his promiſed land, if he had once ſeen the fruitful realms of Sicily and Naples (See Giannone Iſtoria Civile del' Regno di Napoli, tom. ii. p. 245). This raillery, which

which malice has perhaps falsely imputed to Frederick, is inconsistent with truth and piety; yet it must be confessed, that the soil of Palestine does not contain that inexhaustible, and as it were spontaneous, principle of fecundity, which, under the most unfavourable circumstance, has covered with rich harvests the banks of the Nile, the fields of Sicily, or the plains of Poland. The Jordan is the only navigable river of Palestine: a considerable part of the narrow space is occupied, or rather lost, in the *Dead Sea*, whose horrid aspect inspires every sensation of disgust, and countenances every tale of horror. The districts which border on Arabia partake of the sandy quality of the adjacent desert. The face of the country, except the sea-coast and the valley of the Jordan, is covered with mountains, which appear for the most part as naked and barren rocks; and in the neighbourhood of Jerusalem there is a real scarcity of the two elements of earth and water (See Maundrel's Travels, p. 65, and Reland Palestin. tom. i. p. 238—395). These disadvantages, which now operate in their fullest extent, were formerly corrected by the labours of a numerous people, and the active protection of a wise government. The hills were clothed with rich beds of artificial mould, the rain was collected in vast cisterns, a supply

ply of fresh water was conveyed by pipes and aqueducts to the dry lands, the breed of cattle was encouraged in those parts which were not adapted for tillage, and almost every spot was compelled to yield some production for the use of the inhabitants. (See the same testimonies and observations of Maundrel and Reland.)

> ------- Pater ipse colendi
> Haud facilem esse viam voluit, primusque per artem
> Movit agros; curis acuens mortalia corda
> Nec torpere gravi passus SUA REGNA veterno.

Such are the useful victories which have been atchieved by MAN on the lofty mountains of Switzerland, along the rocky coast of Genoa, and upon the barren hills of Palestine; and since Wales has flourished under the influence of English freedom, that rugged country has surely acquired some share of the same industrious merit and the same artificial fertility. Those Critics who interpret the comparison of Palestine and Wales as a tacit libel on the former, are themselves guilty of an unjust satire against the latter, of those countries. Such is the injustice of Mr. Apthorpe and of the anonymous *Gentleman:* but if Mr. Davis (as we may suspect from his name) is himself of Cambrian origin, his patriotism on this occasion has protected me from his zeal.

V.

I ſhall begin this article by the confeſſion of an error which candour might perhaps excuſe, but which my Adverſary magnifies by a pathetic interrogation. "When he tells us, that he "has carefully examined all the original ma-"terials, are we to believe him? or is it his "deſign to try how far the credulity and eaſy "diſpoſition of the age will ſuffer him to pro-"ceed unſuſpected and undiſcovered [6]?" *Quouſque tandem abuteris Catilina patientiâ noſtrâ?*

In ſpeaking of the danger of idolatry, I had quoted the pictoreſque expreſſion of Tertullian, "Recogita ſylvam et quantæ latitant ſpinæ," and finding it marked c. 10 in my Notes, I haſtily, though naturally, added *de Idololatria*, inſtead of *de Corona Militis*, and referred to one Treatiſe of Tertullian inſtead of another [7]. And now let me aſk in my turn, whether Mr. Davis had any real knowledge of the paſſage which I had miſplaced, or whether he made an ungenerous uſe of his advantage, to inſinuate that I had invented or perverted the words of Tertullian? Ignorance is leſs criminal than malice, and I ſhall be ſatisfied if he will plead guilty to the milder charge.

The ſame obſervation may be extended to a paſſage of Le Clerc, which aſſerts, in the

[6] Davis, p. 25. [7] Gibbon, p. 553. Note 40.

cleareſt terms, the ignorance of the more ancient Jews with regard to a future ſtate. Le Clerc lay open before me, but while my eye moved from the book to the paper, I tranſcribed the reference c. 1. ſect. 8. inſtead of ſect. 1. c. 8. from the natural, but erroneous perſuaſion, that *Chapter* expreſſed the larger, and *Section* the ſmaller diviſion[8]: and this difference, of ſuch trifling moment and ſo eaſily rectified, holds a diſtinguiſhed place in the liſt of Miſrepreſentations which adorn Mr. Davis's Table of Contents[9]. But to return to Tertullian.

The *infernal* picture, which I had produced[1] from that vehement writer, which excited the horror of every humane reader, and which even Mr. Davis will not explicitly defend, has furniſhed him with a few critical cavils[2]. Happy ſhould I think myſelf, if the materials of my Hiſtory could be always expoſed to the Examination of the Public; and I ſhall be content with appealing to the impartial Reader, whether my Verſion of this Paſſage is not as fair and as faithful, as the more literal tranſlation which Mr. Davis has exhibited in an oppoſite column. I ſhall only juſtify two

[8] Gibbon, p. 560, Note 58.

[9] Davis, p. 19.

[1] Gibbon, p. 566.

[2] Davis, p. 29—33.

expreſſions which have provoked his indignation. 1. I had obſerved that the zealous African purſues the infernal deſcription in a long variety of affected and unfeeling witticiſms; the inſtances of Gods, of Kings, of Magiſtrates, of Philoſophers, of Poets, of Tragedians, were introduced into my Tranſlation. Thoſe which I had omitted, relate to the Dancers, the Charioteers, and the Wreſtlers; and it is almoſt impoſſible to expreſs thoſe conceits which are connected with the language and manners of the Romans. But the reader will be *ſufficiently* ſhocked, when he is informed that Tertullian alludes to the improvement which the agility of the Dancers, the *red* livery of the Charioteers, and the attitudes of the Wreſtlers, would derive from the effects of fire. "Tunc "hiſtriones cognoſcendi ſolutiores multo per "ignem; tunc ſpectandus Auriga in flammea "rota totus ruber. Tunc Xyſtici contem-"plandi, non in Gymnaſiis, ſed in igne jacu-"lati." 2. I cannot refuſe to anſwer Mr. Davis's very particular queſtion, Why I appeal to Tertullian for the condemnation of the wiſeſt and moſt virtuous of the Pagans? *Becauſe* I am inclined to beſtow that epithet on Trajan and the Antonines, Homer and Euripides, Plato and Ariſtotle, who are all manifeſtly included within the fiery defcription which I had produced.

I am accufed of mifquoting Tertullian ad Scapulam [3], as an evidence that Martyrdoms were lately introduced into Africa [4]. Befides Tertullian, I had quoted from Ruinart (Acta Sincera, p. 84.) the Acts of the Scyllitan Martyrs; and a very moderate knowledge of Ecclefiaftical Hiftory would have informed Mr. Davis, that the two authorities thus connected eftablifh the propofition afferted in my Text. Tertullian, in the above-mentioned Chapter, fpeaks of one of the Proconfuls of Africa, Vigellius Saturninus, "qui *primus hic* gladium in "nos egit;" the Acta Sincera reprefent the fame Magiftrate as the Judge of the Scyllitan Martyrs; and Ruinart, with the confent of the beft Critics, afcribes their fufferings to the perfecution of Severus. Was it my fault if Mr. Davis was incapable of fupplying the intermediate ideas?

Is it likewife neceffary that I fhould juftify the frequent ufe which I have made of Tertullian? His copious writings difplay a lively and interefting picture of the primitive Church, and the fcantinefs of original materials fcarcely left me the liberty of choice. Yet as I was

[3] Davis, p. 35, 36. [4] Gibbon, p 609, Note 172.

fenfible,

ſenſible, that the Montaniſm of Tertullian is the convenient ſcreen which our orthodox Divines have placed before his errors, I have, with peculiar caution, confined myſelf to thoſe works which were compoſed in the more early and ſounder part of his life.

As a collateral juſtification of my frequent appeals to this African Preſbyter, I had introduced, in the third edition of my Hiſtory, two paſſages of Jerom and Prudentius, which prove that Tertullian was the maſter of Cyprian, and that Cyprian was the maſter of the Latin Church[5]. Mr. Davis aſſures me, however, that I ſhould have done better not to have "added this note[6], as I have only accumulated my inaccuracies." One inaccuracy he had indeed detected, an error of the preſs, Hieronym. de Viris illuſtribus, c. 53 for 63; but this advantage is dearly purchaſed by Mr. Davis. Επιδος του διδασκαλου, which he produces as the original words of Cyprian, has a braver and more learned ſound, than *Da magiſtrum*; but the quoting in Greek, a ſentence which was pronounced, and is recorded, in Latin, ſeems to bear the mark of the moſt ridiculous pedantry; unleſs Mr. Davis, conſulting for the firſt time the Works of Jerom, miſtook the Verſion of

[5] Gibbon, p. 566. N. 72.

[6] Davis, p. 145.

Sophronius,

Sophronius, which is printed in the opposite column, for the Text of his original Author. My reference to Prudentius, Hymn. xiii. 100. cannot so easily be justified, as I presumptuously believed that my critics would continue to read till they came to a full stop. I shall now place before them, not the first verse only, but the entire period, which they will find full, express, and satisfactory. The Poet says of St. Cyprian, whom he places in Heaven,

> Nec minus involitat terris, nec ab hoc recedit orbe:
> Disserit, eloquitur, tractat, docet, instruit, prophetat;
> Nec *Libyæ populos* tantum regit, exit usque in ortum
> Solis, et usque obitum; *Gallos* fovet, imbuit *Britannos*,
> Presidet *Hesperiæ*, Christum serit ultimis *Hiberis*.

VI.

On the subject of the imminent dangers which the Apocalypse has so narrowly escaped [7], Mr. Davis accuses me of misrepresenting the sentiments of Sulpicius Severus and Fra-Paolo [8], with this difference, however, that I was incapable of reading or understanding the text of the Latin author; but that I wilfully perverted the sense of the Italian historian. These imputations I shall easily wipe away, by shewing that, in the first instance, I am proba- SULPICIUS SEVERUS AND FRA-PAOLO.

[7] Gibbon, p. 563, 564. N. 67.

[8] Davis, p. 40—44.

bly

bly in the right; and that, in the ſecond, he is certainly in the wrong.

1. The conciſe and elegant Sulpicius, who has been juſtly ſtyled the Chriſtian Salluſt, after mentioning the exile and Revelations of St. John in the iſle of Patmos, obſerves (and ſurely the obſervation is in the language of complaint), "Librum ſacræ Apocalypſis, qui "quidem *a pleriſque* aut ſtulte aut impie non "recipitur, conſcriptum edidit." I am found guilty of ſuppoſing *plerique* to ſignify *the greater number*; whereas Mr. Davis, with Stephens's Dictionary in his hand, is able to prove that *plerique* has not *always* that extenſive meaning, and that a claſſic of good authority has uſed the word in a much more limited and qualified ſenſe. Let the Examiner therefore try to apply his exception to this particular caſe. For my part, *I* ſtand under the protection of the general uſage of the Latin language, and with a ſtrong preſumption in favour of the juſtice of my cauſe, or at leaſt of the innocence and fairneſs of my intentions; ſince I have tranſlated a familiar word, according to its acknowledged and ordinary acceptation.

But, "if I had looked into the paſſage, and "found that Sulpicius Severus there expreſsly "tells us, that the Apocalypſe was the work "of St. John, I could not have committed ſo

"unfortunate

"unfortunate a *blunder*, as to cite this Father
" as saying, That the greater number of Chris-
" tians denied its Canonical authority [9]."
Unfortunate indeed would have been my blunder, had I asserted that the same Christians who denied its Canonical authority, admitted it to be the work of an Apostle. Such indeed was the opinion of Severus himself, and his opinion has obtained the sanction of the Church; but the Christians whom he taxes with folly or impiety for rejecting this sacred book, must have supported their error by attributing the Apocalypse to some uninspired writer; to John the Presbyter, or to Cerinthus the Heretic.

If the rules of grammar and of logic authorise, or at least allow me to translate *plerique* by the *greater number*, the Ecclesiastical History of the fourth century illustrates and justifies this obvious interpretation. From a fair comparison of the populousness and learning of the Greek and Latin Churches, may I not conclude that the former contained the *greater number* of Christians qualified to pass sentence on a mysterious prophecy composed in the Greek language? May I not affirm, on the authority of St. Jerom, that the Apocalypse was generally rejected by the Greek Churches?

9 Davis, p. 270.

"Quod si eam (the Epistle to the Hebrews) "Latinorum consuetudo non recipit inter "Scripturas Canonicas; nec Græcorum Ec- "clesiæ Apocalypsim Johannis eadem libertate "suscipiunt. Et tamen nos utramque suscipi- "mus, nequaqam hujus temporis consuetu- "dinem, sed veterum auctoritatem sequentes." Epistol. ad Dardanum, tom. iii. p. 68.

It is not my design to enter any farther into the controverted history of that famous book; but I am called upon [1] to defend my Remark that the Apocalypse was tacitly excluded from the sacred canon by the council of Laodicea (Canon LX.). To defend my Remark, I need only state the fact in a simple, but more particular manner. The assembled Bishops of Asia, after enumerating all the books of the Old and New Testament which should be read in churches, omit the Apocalypse, and the Apocalypse alone; at a time when it was rejected or questioned by many pious and learned Christians, who might deduce a very plausible argument from the silence of the Synod.

2. When the Council of Trent resolved to pronounce sentence on the Canon of Scripture, the opinion which prevailed, after some debate, was to declare the Latin Vulgate authentic and

[1] By Mr. Davis, p. 41. and by Dr. Chelsum, Remarks, p. 57.

almost infallible; and this sentence, which was guarded by formidable Anathemas, secured all the books of the Old and New Testament which composed that ancient version, " che si " dichiarassero tutti in tutte le parte come si " trovano nella Biblia Latina, esser di Divina " è ugual autorita." (Istoria del Concilio Tridentino, l. ii. p. 147. Helmstadt *(Vicenza)* 1761.) When the merit of that Version was discussed, the majority of the Theologians urged, with confidence and success, that it was absolutely necessary to receive the Vulgate as authentic and inspired, unless they wished to abandon the victory to the Lutherans, and the honours of the Church to the Grammarians. " In contrario della maggior parte dè Teo- " logi era detto . . . . che-questi nuovi Gram- " matici confonderanno ogni cosa, e sarà far- " gli giudici e arbitri della fede; e in luogo " dè Teologi e Canonisti, converrà tener il " primo conto nell' assumere a Vescovati e " Cardinalati dè pedanti." (Istoria del Concilio Tridentino, l. ii. p. 149.) The sagacious Historian, who had studied the Council, and the judicious Le Courayer, who had studied his Author (Histoire du Concile de Trente, tom. i. p. 245. Londres 1736), consider this *ridiculous* reason as the most powerful argument which influenced the debates of the Council: But

Mr. Davis, jealous of the honour of a Synod, which placed tradition on a level with the Bible, affirms that Fra-Paolo has given another more ſubſtantial reaſon on which theſe Popiſh Biſhops built their determination, That after dividing the books under their conſideration into three claſſes; of thoſe which had been always held for divine; of thoſe whoſe authenticity had formerly been doubted, but which by uſe and cuſtom had acquired canonical authority; and of thoſe which had never been properly certified; the Apocalypſe was judiciouſly placed by the Fathers of the Council in the ſecond of theſe claſſes.

The Italian paſſage, which, for that purpoſe, Mr. Davis has alleged at the bottom of his page, is indeed taken from the text of Fra-Paolo; but the reader, who will give himſelf the trouble, or rather the pleaſure, of peruſing that incomparable hiſtorian, will diſcover that Mr. Davis has *only* miſtaken a motion of the oppoſition, for a meaſure of the adminiſtration. He will find, that this critical diviſion, which is ſo erroneouſly aſcribed to the public reaſon of the Council, was no more than the ineffectual propoſal of a temperate minority, which was ſoon over-ruled by a majority of artful Stateſmen, bigotted Monks, and dependent Biſhops.

"We have here an evident proof that Mr. "Gibbon is equally expert in misrepresenting "a modern as an ancient writer, or that he "wilfully conceals the most material reason, "with a design, no doubt, to instil into his "Reader a notion, that the authenticity of the "Apocalypse is built on the slightest foun- "dation[2]."

VII.

I had cautiously observed (for I was apprised of the obscurity of the subject) that the Epistle of Clemens does not lead us to discover any traces of Episcopacy either at Corinth or Rome[3]. In this observation I particularly alluded to the republican form of salutation, "The Church "of God inhabiting Rome, to the Church of "God inhabiting Corinth;" without the least mention of a Bishop or President in either of those ecclesiastical assemblies. CLEMENS.

Yet the piercing eye of Mr. Davis[4] can discover not only traces, but evident proofs, of Episcopacy, in this Epistle of Clemens; and he actually quotes two passages, in which he distinguishes by capital letters the word BISHOPS, whose institution Clemens refers to the Apostles themselves. But can Mr. Davis hope to gain credit by such egregious trifling?

[2] Davis, p. 44. [3] Gibbon, p. 592. N. 110.
[4] Davis, p. 44, 45.

While

While we are searching for the origin of Bishops, not merely as an ecclesiastical title, but as the peculiar name of an order distinct from that of Presbyters, he idly produces a passage, which, by declaring that the Apostles established in every place *Bishops* and *Deacons*, evidently confounds the *Presbyters* with one or other of those two ranks. I have neither inclination nor interest to engage in a controversy which I had considered only in an historical light; but I have already said enough to shew, that there are more traces of a disingenuous mind in Mr. Davis, than of an Episcopal Order in the Epistle of Clemens.

VIII.

EUSEBIUS. Perhaps, on some future occasion, I may examine the historical character of Eusebius; perhaps I may enquire, how far it appears from his words and actions, that the learned Bishop of Cæsarea was averse to the use of fraud, when it was employed in the service of Religion. At present, I am only concerned to defend my own truth and honour, from the reproach of misrepresenting the sense of the Ecclesiastical Historian. Some of the charges of Mr. Davis on this head are so strong, so pointed, so vehemently urged, that he seems to have staked, on the event of the trial, the merits of our

our reſpective characters. If his aſſertions are true, I deſerve the contempt of learned, and the abhorrence of good, men. If they are falſe, * * * * * * *

1. I had remarked, without any malicious intention, that one of the ſeventeen Chriſtians who ſuffered at Alexandria was likewiſe *accuſed* of robbery [5]. Mr. Davis [6] ſeems enraged becauſe I did not add that he was *falſely* accuſed, takes ſome unneceſſary pains to convince me that the Greek word ἐσυκοφαντήθη ſignifies *falſo accuſatus*, and "can hardly think that any one "who had looked into the original, would "dare thus abſolutely to contradict the plain "teſtimony of the author he *pretends* to fol"low." A ſimple narrative of this fact, in the relation of which Mr. Davis has *really* ſuppreſſed ſeveral material circumſtances, will afford the cleareſt juſtification.

Euſebius has preſerved an original letter from Dionyſius Biſhop of Alexandria to Fabius Biſhop of Antioch, in which the former relates the circumſtances of the perſecution which had lately afflicted the capital of Egypt. He

[5] Gibbon, p. 654; N. 75. [6] Davis, p. 61, 62, 63. This ridiculous charge is repeated by another *Sycophant* (in the Greek ſenſe of the word), and forms one of the *valuable* communications, which the learning of a Randolph ſuggeſted to the candour of a Chelſum. See Remarks, p. 209.

allows

allows a rank among the martyrs to one Nemeſion, an Egyptian, who was falſely or maliciouſly accuſed as a companion of robbers. Before the Centurion he juſtified himſelf from this calumny, which did not relate to him; bnt being charged as a Chriſtian, he was brought in chains before the Governor. That unjuſt magiſtrate, after inflicting on Nemeſion *a double meaſure of ſtripes and tortures*, gave orders that he ſhould be *burnt with the robbers*. (Dionyſ. apud Euſeb. l. vi. c. 41.)

It is evident that Dionyſius repreſents the religious ſufferer as innocent of the criminal accuſation which had been falſely brought againſt him. It is no leſs evident, that whatever might be the opinion of the Centurion, the ſupreme magiſtrate conſidered Nemeſion as guilty, and that he affected to ſhew, by the meaſure of his tortures, and by the companions of his execution, that he puniſhed him, not only as a Chriſtian, but as a robber. The evidence againſt Nemeſion, and that which might be produced in his favour, are equally loſt; and the queſtion (which fortunately is of little moment) of his guilt or innocence reſts ſolely on the oppoſite judgments of his eccleſiaſtical and civil ſuperiors. I could eaſily perceive that both the Biſhop and the Governor were actuated by different paſſions and

and prejudices towards the unhappy ſufferer; but it was impoſſible for me to decide which of the two was the moſt likely to indulge his prejudices and paſſions at the expence of truth. In this doubtful ſituation, I conceived that I had acted with the moſt unexceptionable caution, when I contented myſelf with obſerving that Nemeſion was *accuſed*; a circumſtance of a public and authentic nature, in which both parties were agreed.

Mr. Davis will no longer aſk, "what poſ-"ſible evaſion then can Mr. Gibbon have re-"courſe to, to convince the world that I have "*falſely* accuſed *him* of a groſs miſrepreſenta-"tion of Euſebius?"

2. Mr. Davis[7] charges me with falſifying (*falſifying* is a very ſerious word) the teſtimony of Euſebius; becauſe it ſuited my purpoſe to magnify the humanity and even kindneſs of Maxentius towards the afflicted Chriſtians[8]. To ſupport this charge, he produces ſome part of a chapter of Euſebius, the Engliſh in his text, the Greek in his notes, and makes the Eccleſiaſtical Hiſtorian expreſs himſelf in the following terms: "Although Maxentius at "firſt favoured the Chriſtians with a view of "popularity, yet afterwards, being addicted

[7] Davis, p. 64, 65.

[8] Gibbon, p. 693, N. 168.

" to magic, and every other impiety, HE exerted himſelf in perſecuting the Chriſtians, in a more ſevere and deſtructive manner than his predeceſſors had done before him."

If it were in my power to place the volume and chapter of Euſebius (Hiſt. Eccleſ. l. viii. c. 14.) before the eyes of every reader, I ſhould be ſatisfied and ſilent. I ſhould not be under the neceſſity of proteſting, that in the paſſage quoted, or rather abridged, by my adverſary, the ſecond member of the period, which alone contradicts my account of Maxentius, has not the moſt diſtant reference to that odious tyrant. After diſtinguiſhing the mild conduct which *he* affected towards the Chriſtians, Euſebius proceeds to animadvert with becoming ſeverity on the general vices of his reign; the rapes, the murders, the oppreſſion, the promiſcuous maſſacres, which I had faithfully related in their proper place, and in which the Chriſtians, not in their religious, but in their civil capacity, muſt occaſionally have ſhared with the reſt of his unhappy ſubjects. The Eccleſiaſtical Hiſtorian then makes a tranſition to *another tyrant*, the cruel Maximin, who carried away from his friend and ally Maxentius the prize of ſuperior wickedneſs; for HE was addicted to magic arts, and was a cruel perſecutor of the Chriſtians. The evidence of words and facts,

the

the plain meaning of Eusebius, the concurring testimony of Cæcilius or Lactantius, and the superfluous authority of Versions and Commentators, establish beyond the reach of doubt or cavil, that Maximin, and not Maxentius, is stigmatized as a persecutor, and that Mr. Davis alone has deserved the reproach of *falsifying* the testimony of Eusebius.

Let him examine the chapter on which he founds his accusation. If in that moment his feelings are not of the most painful and humiliating kind, he must indeed be an object of pity!

3. *A gross blunder* is imputed to me by this polite antagonist[9], for quoting, under the name of Jerom, the Chronicle which I ought to have described as the work and property of Eusebius[1]; and Mr. Davis kindly points out the occasion of my blunder, That it was the consequence of my looking no farther than Dodwell for this remark, and of not rightly understanding his reference. Perhaps the Historian of the Roman Empire may be credited; when he affirms that he frequently consulted a Latin Chronicle of the affairs of that Empire; and he may the sooner be credited, if he shews that he knows something more of this Chronicle besides the name and the title-page.

[9] Davis, p. 66. [1] Gibbon, p. 673, N. 125.

Mr. Davis, who talks ſo familiarly of the Chronicle of Euſebius, will be ſurpriſed to hear that the Greek original no longer exiſts. Some chronological fragments, which had ſucceſſively paſſed through the hands of Africanus and Euſebius, are ſtill extant, though in a very corrupt and mutilated ſtate, in the compilations of Syncellus and Cedrenus. They have been collected, and diſpoſed by the labour and ingenuity of Joſeph Scaliger; but that proud Critic, always ready to applaud his own ſucceſs, did not flatter himſelf, that he had reſtored the hundredth part of the genuine Chronicle of Euſebius. "Ex eo *(Syncello)* omnia "Euſebiana excerpſimus quæ quidem deprehendere potuimus; quæ, quanquam ne centeſima quidem pars eorum eſſe videtur quæ "ab Euſebio relicta ſunt, aliquod tamen juſtum "volumen explere poſſunt." (Joſ. Scaliger Animadverſiones in Græca Euſebii in Theſauro Temporum, p. 401. Amſtelod. 1658.) While the Chronicle of Euſebius was perfect and entire, the ſecond book was tranſlated into Latin by Jerom, with the freedom, or rather licence, which that voluminous Author, as well as his friend or enemy Rufinus, always aſſumed. "Plurima in vertendo mutat, infulcit, præterit," ſays Scaliger himſelf, in the Prolegomena, p. 22. In the perſecution of Aurelian, which has ſo much

much offended Mr. Davis, we are able to diſtinguiſh the work of Euſebius from that of Jerom, by comparing the expreſſions of the Eccleſiaſtical Hiſtory with thoſe of the Chronicle. The former affirms, that, towards the end of his reign, Aurelian was moved by ſome councils to excite a perſecution againſt the Chriſtians; that his deſign occaſioned a great and general rumour; but that when the letters were prepared, and as it were ſigned, Divine Juſtice diſmiſſed him from the world. Ηδη τισι βȢλαις ως αν διωγμον καθ' ἡμων εγειρειεν ανεκινειτο. πολυς τε ην ὁ παρα πασι περι τȢτȢ λογος. μελλοντα δε ηδη και σχεδον ειπειν τοις καθ' ἡμων γραμμασιν υποσημειȢμενον, θεια μετεισιν δικη. Euſeb. Hiſt. Eccleſ. l. vii. c. 30. Whereas the Chronicle relates, that Aurelian was killed after he had excited or moved a perſecution againſt the Chriſtians, "cum adverſum "nos perſecutionem moviſſet."

From this manifeſt difference I aſſume a right to aſſert; firſt, that the expreſſion of the Chronicle of *Jerom*, which is always proper, became in this inſtance neceſſary; and ſecondly, that the language of the Fathers is ſo ambiguous and incorrect, that we are at a loſs to determine how far Aurelian had carried his intention before he was aſſaſſinated. I have neither perverted the *fact*; nor have I been guilty of *a gross blunder*.

IX.

JUSTIN MARTYR.

"The persons accused of Christianity had "a convenient time allowed them to settle "their domestic concerns, and to prepare their "answer[1]." This observation had been suggested, partly by a general expression of Cyprian (de Lapsis, p. 88. Edit. Fell. Amstelod. 1700), and more especially by the second Apology of Justin Martyr, who gives a particular and curious example of this legal delay.

The expressions of Cyprian, "dies negan-"tibus præstitutus, &c." which Mr. Davis most prudently suppresses, are illustrated by Mosheim in the following words: "Primum qui delati "erant aut suspecti, illis certum dierum spa-"tium judex definiebat, quo decurrente, se-"cum deliberare poterant, utrum profiteri "Christum an negare mallent; *exploranda fidei "præfiniebantur dies*, per hoc tempus liberi "manebant in domibus suis; nec impediebat "aliquis quod ex consequentibus apparet, ne "fugâ sibi consulerent. Satis hoc erat huma-"num." (De Rebus Christianis ante Constantinum, p. 480.) The practice of Egypt was sometimes more expeditious and severe; but

[1] Gibbon, p. 663.

this

this humane indulgence was ſtill allowed in Africa during the perſecution of Decius.

But my appeal to Juſtin Martyr is encountered by Mr. Davis with the following declaration[z]: "The reader will obſerve, that Mr. "Gibbon does not make any reference to any "ſection or diviſion of this part of Juſtin's work; "with what view we may ſhrewdly ſuſpect, "when I tell him, that after an accurate peruſal "of the whole ſecond Apology, I can boldly "affirm, that the following inſtance is the only "one that bears the moſt diſtant ſimilitude to "what Mr. Gibbon relates as above on the "authority of Juſtin. What I find in Juſtin "is as follows: "A woman being converted "to Chriſtianity, is afraid to aſſociate with her "huſband, becauſe he is an abandoned reprobate, leſt ſhe ſhould partake of his ſins. Her "huſband, not being able to accuſe *her*, vents "his rage in this manner on one Ptolemæus, "a teacher of Chriſtianity, and who had con"verted her, *&c.*" Mr. Davis then proceeds to relate the ſeverities inflicted on Ptolemæus, who made a frank and inſtant profeſſion of his faith; and he ſternly exclaims, that if I take every opportunity of paſſing encomiums on the humanity of Roman magiſtrates, it is incum-

[z] Davis, p. 71, 72.

bent

bent on me to produce better evidence than this.

His demand may be eaſily ſatisfied, and I need only for that purpoſe tranſcribe and tranſlate the words of Juſtin, which *immediately* precede the Greek quotation alleged at the bottom of my adverſary's page. I am poſſeſſed of two editions of Juſtin Martyr, that of Cambridge, 1768, in 8vo, by Dr. Aſhton, who only publiſhed the two Apologies; and that of all his works, publiſhed in fol. Paris, 1742, by the Benedictines of the Congregation of St. Maar: the following curious paſſage may be found, p. 164, of the former, and p. 89 of the latter Edition. *κατηγοριαν πεποιηται, λεγων αυτην χριστιανην ειναι, και ἡ μεν βιβλιδιον σοι τω αυτοκρατορι αναδεδωκε, προτερον συγχωρηθηναι αυτῃ διοικησασθαι τα εαυτής αξιȣσα. επειτα απολογησασθαι περι τȣ κατηγορηματος, μετα την των πραγματων αυτης διοικησιν. και συνεχωρήσας τȣτο.* "He brought an accuſation "against her, ſaying, that ſhe was a Chriſtian. "But ſhe preſented a petition to the Emperor, "praying that ſhe might firſt be allowed to "ſettle her domeſtic concerns; and promiſing, "that, after ſhe had ſettled them, ſhe would "then put in her anſwer to the accuſation. "This you granted."

I diſdain to add a ſingle reflection; nor ſhall I qualify the conduct of my adverſary with any

of

of thoſe harſh epithets, which might be interpreted as the expreſſions of reſentment, though I ſhould be conſtrained to uſe them as the only words in the Engliſh language, which could accurately repreſent my cool and unprejudiced ſentiments.

X.

In ſtating the toleration of Chriſtianity during the greateſt part of the reign of Diocletian, I had obſerved [3], that the principal officers of the palace, whoſe names and functions were particularly ſpecified, enjoyed, with their wives and children, the free exerciſe of the Chriſtian religion. Mr. Davis twice affirms [4], in the moſt deliberate manner, that this pretended fact, which is aſſerted on the ſole authority, is contradicted by the poſitive evidence, of Lactantius. In both theſe *affirmations* Mr. Davis is inexcuſably miſtaken. LACTANTIUS.

1. When the ſtorms of perſecution aroſe, the Prieſts, who were offended by the ſign of the Croſs, obtained an order from the Emperor, that the profane, the Chriſtians, who accompanied him to the Temple, ſhould be compelled to offer ſacrifice; and this incident is mentioned by the Rhetorician, to whom I ſhall not at preſent refuſe the name of Lactantius. The act of

[3] Gibbon, p. 676. N. 133, 134. [4] Davis, p. 75, 76.

idolatry, which, at the expiration of eighteen years, was required of the officers of Diocletian, is a manifest proof that their religious freedom had hitherto been inviolate, except in the single instance of waiting on their master to the Temple; a service less criminal than the profane compliance for which the Minister of the King of Syria solicited the permission of the Prophet of Israel.

2. The reference which I made to Lactantius expressly pointed out this exception to their freedom. But the proof of the toleration was built on a different testimony, which my disingenuous adversary has concealed; an ancient and curious instruction, composed by Bishop Theonas, for the use of Lucian, and the other Christian eunuchs of the palace of Diocletian. This authentic piece was published in the Spicilegium of Dom Luc d'Acheri; as I had not the opportunity of consulting the original, I was contented with quoting it on the faith of Tillemont, and the reference to it immediately precedes (ch. xvi. note 133.) the citation of Lactantius (note 134).

Mr. Davis may now answer his own question, "What apology can be made for thus asserting, on the sole authority of Lactantius, "facts which Lactantius so expressly denies?"

XI.

DION CASSIUS.

"I have already given a curious instance "of our Author's asserting, on the authority of "Dion Cassius, a fact not mentioned by that "Historian. I shall now produce a very sin- "gular proof of his endeavouring to conceal "from us a passage really contained in him [4]." Nothing but the angry vehemence with which these charges are urged, could engage me to take the least notice of them. In themselves they are doubly contemptible; they are trifling, and they are false.

1. Mr. Davis [5] had imputed to me as a crime, that I had mentioned, on the sole testimony of Dion (l. lxviii. p. 1145.), the spirit of rebellion which inflamed the Jews, from the reign of Nero to that of Antoninus Pius [6], whilst the passage of that Historian is confined to an insurrection in Cyprus and Cyrene, which broke out within that period. The Reader who will cast his eye on the Note (ch. xvi. note 1.), which is supported by that quotation from Dion, will discover that it related only to *this* particular fact. The general position, which is indeed too notorious to require any proof, I had carefully justified in the course of the same paragraph; partly by another reference to Dion Cassius, partly by an

[4] Davis, p. 83. [5] Id. p. 11. [6] Gibbon, p. 622.

allusion to the well-known History of Josephus, and partly by *several* quotations from the learned and judicious Basnage, who has explained, in the most satisfactory manner, the principles and conduct of the rebellious Jews.

2. The passage of Dion, which I am accused of endeavouring to conceal, might perhaps have remained invisible, even to the piercing eye of Mr. Davis, if *I* had not carefully reported it in its proper place[7]: and it was in my power to report it, without being guilty of any *inconsiderate contradiction.* I had observed, that, in the large history of Dion Cassius, Xiphilin had not been able to discover the name of *Christians;* yet I afterwards quote a passage in which Marcia, the favourite Concubine of Commodus, is celebrated as the Patroness of the *Christians.* Mr. Davis has transcribed my quotation, but *he* has concealed the important words which I now distinguish by Italics (ch. xvi. note 106. Dion Cassius, *or rather his abbreviator Xiphilin,* l. lxxii. p. 1206.) The reference is fairly made and cautiously qualified: I am already secure from the imputations of fraud or inconsistency; and the opinion which attributes the last-mentioned passage to the Abbreviator, rather than to the original Historian, may be supported by the most unexception-

[7] Gibbon, p. 667. N. 107.

able

able authorities. I shall protect myself by those of Reimar (in his Edition of Dion Cassius, tom. ii. p. 1207. note 34.), and of Dr. Lardner; and shall only transcribe the words of the latter, in his Collection of Jewish and Heathen Testimonies, vol. iii. p. 57.

" This paragraph I rather think to be Xi-" philin's than Dion's. The style at least is " Xiphilin's. In the other passages before " quoted, Dion speaks of *Impiety*, or *Atheism*, " or *Judaism*; but never useth the word *Chris-" tians.* Another thing that may make us " doubt whether this observation be entirely " Dion's, is the phrase, " it is related (ἱστο-" ρεῖται)." For at the beginning of the reign " of Commodus, he says, " These things, " and what follows, I write not from the report " of others, but from my own knowledge and " observation." However, the sense may be " Dion's; but I wish we had also his style with-" out any adulteration." For my own part, I must, in my private opinion, ascribe even the sense of this passage to Xiphilin. The *Monk* might eagerly collect and insert an anecdote which related to the domestic history of the church; but the religion of a courtezan must have appeared an object of very little moment in the eyes of a *Roman Consul*, who, at least in every other part of his history, disdained or neglected

neglected to mention the name of the Christians.

"What shall we say now? Do we not discover the name of Christians in the History of Dion? With what *assurance* then can Mr. Gibbon, after asserting a fact manifestly *untrue*, lay claim to the merits of diligence and accuracy, the indispensable duty of an Historian? Or can he expect us to credit his assertion, that he has carefully examined all the original materials[8]?"

Mr. Gibbon may still maintain the character of an Historian; but it is difficult to conceive how Mr. Davis will support his pretensions, if he aspires to that of a Gentleman.

I almost hesitate whether I should take any notice of another ridiculous charge which Mr. Davis includes in the article of Dion Cassius. My adversary owns, that I have occasionally produced the several passages of the Augustan History which relate to the Christians; but he fiercely contends that they amount to more than *six lines*[9]. I really have not measured them: nor did I mean that loose expression as a precise and definite number. If, on a nicer survey, those short hints, when they are brought together, should be found to exceed six

[8] Davis, p. 83. [9] Gibbon, p. 634. N. 24.

of

of the long lines of my folio edition, I am content that my critical Antagonist should substitute eight, or ten, or twelve, lines: nor shall I think either my learning or my veracity much interested in this important alteration.

XII.

After a short description of the unworthy conduct of those Apostates who, in a time of persecution, deserted the Faith of Christ, I produced the evidence of a Pagan Proconsul[1], and of two christian Bishops, Pliny, Dionysius of Alexandria, and Cyprian. And here the unforgiving Critic remarks, "That Pliny has "not particularized that difference of conduct "(in the different Apostates) which Mr. Gibbon here describes: yet his name stands at "the head of those Authors whom he has "cited on the occasion. It is allowed indeed "that this distinction is made by the other "Authors; but as Pliny, the first referred to "by Mr. Gibbon, gives him no cause or reason to use *them*," (I cannot help Mr. Davis's bad English) "it is certainly very reprehensible in our Author, thus to confound "their testimony, and to make a needless and "improper reference[2]." PLINY, &c.

[1] Gibbon, p. 664. N. 102.   [2] Davis, p. 87, 88.

A criticism of this sort can only tend to expose Mr. Davis's total ignorance of historical composition. The Writer who aspires to the name of Historian, is obliged to consult a variety of original testimonies, each of which, taken separately, is perhaps imperfect and partial. By a judicious re-union and arrangement of these dispersed materials, he endeavours to form a consistent and interesting narrative. Nothing ought to be inserted which is not proved by some of the witnesses; but their evidence must be so intimately blended together, that as it is unreasonable to expect that each of them should vouch for the whole, so it would be impossible to define the boundaries of their respective property. Neither Pliny, nor Dionysius, nor Cyprian, mention *all* the circumstances and *distinctions* of the conduct of the Christian Apostates; but if any of them was withdrawn, the account which I have given would, in some instance, be defective.

Thus much I thought necessary to say, as several of the subsequent *misrepresentations* of Orosius, of Bayle, of Fabricius, of Gregory of Tours, &c. [3], which provoked the fury of Mr. Davis, are derived only from the ignorance of this common historical principle.

[3] Davis, p. 88. 90. 137.

Another

Another claſs of Miſrepreſentations, which my Adverſary urges with the ſame degree of vehemence (See in particular thoſe of Juſtin, Diodorus Siculus, and even Tacitus), requires the ſupport of another principle, which has not yet been introduced into the art of criticiſm; *that* when a modern hiſtorian appeals to the authority of the ancients for the truth of any particular fact; he makes himſelf anſwerable, I know not to what extent, for all the circumjacent errors or inconſiſtencies of the authors whom he has quoted.

XIII.

I am accuſed of throwing out a falſe accuſation againſt this Father[3], becauſe I had obſerved[4] that Ignatius, defending againſt the Gnoſtics the reſurrection of Chriſt, employs a vague and doubtful tradition, inſtead of quoting the certain teſtimony of the Evangeliſts: and this obſervation was juſtified by a remarkable paſſage of Ignatius, in his Epiſtle to the Smyrnæans, which I cited according to the volume and the page of the beſt edition of the Apoſtolical Fathers, publiſhed at Amſterdam, 1724, in two volumes in folio. The Criticiſm of Mr. Davis is announced by one of thoſe ſolemn declarations which leave not any IGNATIUS.

[3] Davis, p. 100, 101. [4] Gibbon, p. 551. Note 35.

refuge, if they are convicted of falsehood. "I cannot find any passage that bears the least "affinity to what Mr. Gibbon observes, in the "whole Epistle, which I have read over more "than once."

I had already marked the *situation*; nor is it in my power to prove the *existence*, of this passage, by any other means than by producing the words of the original. Εγω γαρ και μετα την αναστασιν εν σαρκι αυτον οιδα και πιστευω οντα, και οτε προς τους περι Πετρον ηλθεν, εφη αυτοις, λαβετε, ψυλαφησατε με, και ιδετε οτι ουκ' ειμι δαιμονιον ασωματον. και ευθυς αυτου ἥψαντο, και επιστευσαν. "I have known, and I believe, that after his "resurrection likewise he existed in the flesh: "And when he came to Peter, and to the rest, "he said unto them, Take, handle me, and "see that I am not an incorporeal dæmon or "spirit. And they touched him, and believ-"ed." The faith of the Apostles confuted the impious error of the Gnostics, which attributed only the *appearances* of a human body to the Son of God: and it was the great object of Ignatius, in the last moments of his life, to secure the Christians of Asia from the snares of those dangerous Heretics. According to the tradition of the modern Greeks, Ignatius was the child whom Jesus received into his arms (See Tillemont Mem. Eccles. tom. ii. part ii. p. 43.);

p. 43.); yet as he could scarcely be old enough to remember the resurrection of the Son of God, he must have derived his knowledge *either* from our present Evangelists, *or* from some Apocryphal Gospel, *or* from some unwritten tradition.

1. The Gospels of St. Luke and St. John would undoubtedly have supplied Ignatius with the most invincible proofs of the reality of the body of Christ, when he appeared to the Apostles after his resurrection; but neither of those Gospels contain the characteristic words of ουκ δαιμονιον ασωματον, and the important circumstance that either Peter, or *those* who were with Peter, touched the body of Christ and believed. Had the saint designed to quote the Evangelist on a very nice subject of controversy, he would not surely have exposed himself, by an inaccurate, or rather by a false, reference, to the just reproaches of the Gnostics. On this occasion, therefore, Ignatius did not employ, as he might have done, against the Heretics, the certain testimony of the Evangelists.

2. Jerom, who cites this remarkable passage from the Epistle of Ignatius to the Smyrnæans (See Catalog. Script. Eccles. in Ignatio, tom. i. p. 273. edit. Erasm. Basil, 1537), is of opinion that it was taken from the *Gospel* which he himself

ſelf had lately tranſlated: and *this*, from the compariſon of two other paſſages in the ſame Work (in Jacob. et in Matthæo, p. 264), appears to have been the Hebrew Goſpel, which was uſed by the Nazarenes of Beræa, as the genuine compoſition of St. Matthew. Yet Jerom mentions another Copy of this Hebrew Goſpel (ſo different from the Greek Text), which was extant in the library formed at Cæſarea, by the care of Pamphilus: whilſt the learned Euſebius, the friend of Pamphilus and the Biſhop of Cæſarea, very frankly declares (Hiſt. Eccleſ. l. iii. c. 36.), that *he* is ignorant from whence Ignatius borrowed thoſe words, which are the ſubject of the preſent Inquiry.

3. The doubt which remains, is only whether he took them from an Apocryphal Book, or from *unwritten tradition:* and I thought myſelf ſafe from every ſpecies of Critics, when I embraced the rational ſentiment of Caſaubon and Pearſon. I ſhall produce the words of the Biſhop. "Præterea iterum obſervandum eſt, "quod de hác re ſcripſit Iſaacus Caſaubonus, "*Quinetiam fortaſſe verius, non ex Evangelio* "*Hebraico, Ignatium illa verba deſcripſiſſe, verum* "*traditionem allegaſſe non ſcriptam, quæ poſtea in* "*literas fuerit relata, et Hebraico Evangelio, quod* "*Matthæo tribuebant, inſerta.* Et hoc quidem "mihi multo veriſimilius videtur." (Pearſon. Vindiciæ

Vindiciæ Ignatianæ, part ii. c. ix. p. 396. in tom. ii. Patr. Apoſtol.)

I may now ſubmit to the judgment of the Public, whether I have looked into the Epiſtle which I cite with ſuch a parade of learning, and *how profitably* Mr. Davis has read it over more than once.

XIV.

The learning and judgment of Moſheim had been of frequent uſe in the courſe of my Hiſtorical Inquiry, and I had not been wanting in proper expreſſions of gratitude. My vexatious Adverſary is always ready to ſtart from his ambuſcade, and to haraſs my march by a mode of attack, which cannot eaſily be reconciled with the laws of honourable war. The greateſt part of the Miſrepreſentations of Moſheim, which Mr. Davis has imputed to me [s], are of ſuch a nature, that I muſt indeed be humble, if I could perſuade myſelf to beſtow a moment of ſerious attention on them. *Whether* Moſheim could prove that an abſolute community of goods was not eſtabliſhed among the firſt Chriſtians of Jeruſalem; *whether* he ſuſpected the purity of the Epiſtles of Ignatius; *whether* he cenſured Dr. Middleton with tem- MOSHEIM.

[s] Davis, p. 95—97. 104—107. 114—132.

per or indignation (in this cauſe I muſt challenge Mr. Davis as an incompetent judge); *whether* he corroborates the *whole* of my deſcription of the prophetic office; *whether* he ſpeaks with approbation of the humanity of Pliny, and *whether* he attributed the ſame ſenſe to the *malefica* of Suetonius, and the *exitiabilis* of Tacitus? Theſe queſtions, even as Mr. Davis has ſtated them, lie open to the judgment of every reader, and the ſuperfluous obſervations which I could make, would be an abuſe of their time and of my own. As little ſhall I think of conſuming their patience, by examining whether Le Clerc and Moſheim *labour* in the interpretation of ſome texts of the Fathers, and particularly of a paſſage of Irenæus, which ſeem to favour the pretenſions of the Roman Biſhop. The material part of the paſſage of Irenæus conſiſts of about *four lines*; and in order to ſhew that the interpretations of Le Clerc and Moſheim are not *laboured*, Mr. Davis abridges them as much as poſſible in the ſpace of *twelve pages*. I know not whether the peruſal of my Hiſtory will juſtify the ſuſpicion of Mr. Davis, that I am ſecretly inclined to the intereſt of the Pope: but I cannot diſcover how the Proteſtant cauſe can be affected, if Irenæus in the ſecond, or Palavicini in the ſeventeenth century, were tempted, by any private

views,

views, to countenance in their writings the system of ecclesiastical dominion, which has been pursued in every age by the aspiring Bishops of the Imperial city. Their conduct was adapted to the revolutions of the Christian Republic, but the same spirit animated the haughty breasts of Victor the First, and of Paul the Fifth.

There still remain one or two of these imputed Misrepresentations, which appear, and indeed only appear, to merit a little more attention. In stating the opinion of Mosheim with regard to the progress of the Gospel, Mr. Davis boldly declares, "that I have *altered the* "*truth* of Mosheim's history, that I might "have an opportunity of contradicting the be-"lief and wishes of the Fathers[6]." In other words, I have been guilty of uttering a malicious falsehood.

I had endeavoured to mitigate the sanguine expression of the Fathers of the second century, who had too hastily diffused the light of Christianity over every part of the globe, by observing, as an undoubted fact, "that the Bar-"barians of Scythia and Germany, who sub-"verted the Roman Monarchy, were involved "in the errors of Paganism; and that even "the conquest of Iberia, of Armenia, or of

[6] Davis, p. 127.

"Æthiopia,

" Æthiopia, was not attempted with any de- " gree of ſucceſs, till the ſcepter was in the " hands of an orthodox Emperor[7]." I had referred the curious reader to the fourth century of Moſheim's General Hiſtory of the Church: Now Mr. Davis has diſcovered, and can prove, from that excellent work, " that " Chriſtianity, not long after its firſt riſe, had " been introduced into the leſs as well as " greater Armenia; that part of the Goths, " who inhabited Thracia, Mæſia, and Dacia, " had received the Chriſtian religion long be- " fore this century; and that Theophilus, their " Biſhop, was preſent at the Council of " Nice[8]."

On this occaſion, the reference was made to a popular work of Moſheim, for the ſatisfaction of the reader, that he might obtain the general view of the progreſs of Chriſtianity in the fourth century, which I had gradually acquired by ſtudying with ſome care the Eccleſiaſtic Antiquities of the Nations beyond the limits of the Roman Empire. If I had reaſonably ſuppoſed that the reſult of our common inquiries muſt be the ſame, ſhould I have deſerved a very harſh cenſure for my unſuſpecting confidence? Or if I had declined the invidious taſk

[7] Gibbon, p. 611, 612. [8] Davis, p. 126, 127.

of

of ſeparating a few immaterial errors, from a juſt and judicious repreſentation, might not my reſpect for the name and merit of Moſheim, have claimed ſome indulgence? But I diſdain thoſe excuſes, which only a candid adverſary would allow. I can meet Mr. Davis on the hard ground of controverſy, and retort on his own head the charge of concealing a part of the truth. He himſelf has dared to ſuppreſs the words of my text, which immediately followed his quotation. "Before that time the various "accidents of war and commerce might indeed "diffuſe an imperfect knowledge of the Goſpel "among the tribes of Caledonia, and among "the borderers of the Rhine, the Danube, "and the Euphrates;" and Mr. Davis has likewiſe ſuppreſſed one of the juſtificatory Notes on this paſſage, which expreſsly points out the time and circumſtances of the firſt Gothic converſions. Theſe exceptions, which I had cautiouſly inſerted, and Mr. Davis has cautiouſly concealed, are ſuperfluous for the provinces of Thrace, Mæſia, and the Leſſer Armenia, which were contained within the precincts of the Roman Empire. They allow an ample ſcope for the more early converſion of ſome independent diſtricts of Dacia and the Greater Armenia, which bordered on the Danube and Euphrates; and the entire ſenſe of this paſſage, which Mr.

Davis first mutilates and then attacks, is perfectly consistent with the original text of the learned Mosheim.

And yet I will fairly confess, that, after a nicer inquiry into the epoch of the Armenian Church, I am not satisfied with the accuracy of my own expression. The assurance that the first Christian King, and the first Archbishop, Tiridates, and St. Gregory the Illuminator, were still alive several years after the death of Constantine, inclined me to believe, that the conversion of Armenia was posterior to the auspicious Revolution, which had given the scepter of Rome to the hands of an orthodox Emperor. But I had not enough considered the two following circumstances. 1. I might have recollected the dates assigned by Moses of Chorene, who, on this occasion, may be regarded as a competent witness. Tiridates ascended the throne of Armenia in the third year of Diocletian (Hist. Armeniæ, l. ii. c. 79. p. 207.), and St. Gregory, who was invested with the Episcopal character in the seventeenth year of Tiridates, governed almost thirty years the Church of Armenia, and disappeared from the world in the forty-sixth year of the reign of the same Prince. (Hist. Armeniæ, l. ii. c. 88. p. 224, 225.) The consecration of St. Gregory must therefore be placed A. D. 303. and the

the conversion of the King and kingdom was soon atchieved by that successful missionary.

2. The unjust and inglorious war which Maximin undertook against the Armenians, the ancient faithful allies of the Republic, was evidently derived from a motive of superstitious zeal. The historian Eusebius (Hist. Eccles. l. ix. c. 8. p. 448. edit. Cantab.) considers the pious Armenians as a nation of Christians, who bravely defended themselves from the hostile oppression of an idolatrous tyrant. Instead of maintaining "that the conversion of Armenia "was not attempted with any degree of success "till the scepter was in the hands of an ortho-"dox Emperor," I ought to have observed, that the seeds of the faith were deeply sown during the season of the last and greatest persecution, that many Roman exiles might assist the labours of Gregory, and that the renowned Tiridates, the hero of the East, may dispute with Constantine the honour of being the first Sovereign who embraced the Christian religion.

In a future edition, I shall rectify an expression which, in strictness, can only be applied to the kingdoms of Iberia and Æthiopia. Had the error been exposed by Mr. Davis himself, I should not have been ashamed to correct it; but *I am* ashamed at being reduced to contend with an adverſary who is unable to diſcover, or to improve, his own advantages.

But, inſtead of proſecuting any inquiry from whence the Public might have gained inſtruction, and himſelf credit, Mr. Davis chuſes to perplex his readers with ſome angry cavils about the progreſs of the Goſpel in the ſecond century. What does he mean to eſtabliſh or to refute? Have I denied, that before the end of that period Chriſtianity was very widely diffuſed both in the Eaſt and in the Weſt? Has not Juſtin Martyr affirmed, without exception or limitation, that it was already preached to *every* nation on the face of the earth? Is that propoſition true at preſent? Could it be true in the time of Juſtin? Does not Moſheim acknowledge the exaggeration? "Demus, nec enim "quæ in oculos incurrunt infitiari audemus, "eſſe in his verbis exaggerationis nonnihil. "Certum enim eſt diu poſt Juſtini ætatem, "multas orbis terrarum gentes cognitione "Chriſti caruiſſe." (Moſheim de Rebus Chriſtianis, p. 203.) Does he not expoſe (p. 205.), with becoming ſcorn and indignation, the falſehood and vanity of the hyperboles of Tertullian? "bonum hominem æſtu imaginationis "elatum non ſatis adtendiſſe ad ea quæ litteris "conſignabat."

The

The high esteem which Mr. Davis expresses for the writings of Mosheim, would alone convince me how little he has read them, since he must have been perpetually offended and disgusted by a train of thinking, the most repugnant to his own. His jealousy, however, for the honour of Mosheim, provokes him to arraign the boldness of Mr. Gibbon who presumes *falsely* to charge such an eminent man with *unjustifiable assertions* [9]. I might observe, that my style, which on this occasion was more modest and moderate, has acquired, perhaps undesignedly, an illiberal cast from the rough hand of Mr. Davis. But as my veracity is impeached, I may be less solicitous about my politeness; and though I have repeatedly declined the fairest opportunities of correcting the errors of my predecessors, yet, as long as I have truth on my side, I am not easily daunted by the names of the most eminent men.

The assertion of Mosheim, which did not seem to be justified [1] by the authority of Lactantius, was, that the wife and daughter of Diocletian, Prisca and *Valeria*, had been privately *baptized*. Mr. Davis is sure that the words of Mosheim, "Christianis sacris clam "initiata," need not be confined to the rite

[9] Davis, p. 131. [1] Gibbon, p. 676, Note 132.

of

of baptism; and he is equally sure, that the reference to Mosheim does not lead us to discover even the name of Valeria. In both these assurances he is grossly mistaken; but it is the misfortune of controversy, that an error may be committed in three or four words, which cannot be rectified in less than thirty or forty lines.

1. The true and the sole meaning of the Christian initiation, one of the familiar and favourite allusions of the Fathers of the fourth century, is clearly explained by the exact and laborious Bingham. "The baptized were "also styled οἱ μεμυημενοι, which the Latins "call *initiati*, the initiated, that is, admitted to "the use of the *sacred* offices, and knowledge "of the *sacred* mysteries of the Christian Religion. "Hence came that form of speaking so fre-"quently used by St. Chrysostom, and other "ancient writers, when they touched upon "any doctrines or mysteries which the Cate-"chumens understood not, ισασιν οἱ μεμυημενοι, "the initiated know what is spoken. St. "Ambrose writes a book to these *initiati*; "Isidore of Pelusium and Hesychius call "them μυσται and μυσταγωγητοι. Whence the "Catechumens have the contrary names, "Αμυστοι, Αμυητοι, Αμυσταγωγητοι, the uniniti-"ated or unbaptized." (Antiquities of the

2 Christian

Christian Church, l. i. c. 4. N° 2. vol. i. p. 11. fol. edit.) Had I presumed to suppose that Mosheim was capable of employing a technical expression in a loose and equivocal sense, I should indeed have violated the respect which I have always entertained for his learning and abilities.

2. But Mr. Davis cannot discover in the text of Mosheim the name of Valeria. In that case Mosheim would have suffered another slight inaccuracy to drop from his pen, as the passage of Lactantius, "sacrificio pollui coë-"git," on which he founds his assertion, includes the names both of Prisca and Valeria. But I am not reduced to the necessity of accusing another in my own defence. Mosheim has properly and expresly declared that Valeria imitated the pious example of her mother Prisca, "Gener Diocletiani uxorem habebat *Vale-"riam* matris exemplum pietate erga Deum "imitantem et a cultu fictorum Numinum "alienam." (Mosheim, p. 913.) Mr. Davis has a bad habit of greedily snapping at the first words of a reference, without giving himself the trouble of going to the end of the page or paragraph.

These trifling and peevish cavils would, perhaps, have been confounded with some criticisms of the same stamp, on which I had bestowed a slight,

slight, though sufficient notice, in the beginning of this article of Mosheim, had not my attention been awakened by a peroration worthy of Tertullian himself, if Tertullian had been devoid of eloquence as well as of moderation— " Much less does the Christian Mosheim give " our *infidel Historian* any pretext for inserting " that *illiberal malignant insinuation*, " That " Christianity has, in every age, acknowledged " its important obligations to FEMALE devo- " tion;" the remark is truly *contemptible*[a]."

It is not my design to fill whole pages with a tedious enumeration of the many illustrious examples of female Saints, who, in every age, and almost in every country, have promoted the interest of Christianity. Such instances will readily offer themselves to those who have the slightest knowledge of Ecclesiastical History; nor is it necessary that I should remind them how much the charms, the influence, the devotion of Clotilda, and of her great-grand-daughter Bertha, contributed to the conversion of France and England. Religion may accept, without a blush, the services of the purest and most gentle portion of the human species: but there are some advocates who would disgrace Christianity, if Christianity

[a] Davis, p. 132.

could

could be disgraced, by the manner in which they defend her cause.

XV.

As I could not readily procure the works of Gregory of Nyssa, I borrowed[3] from the accurate and indefatigable Tillemont, a passage in the Life of Gregory Thaumaturgus, or the Wonder-worker, which affirmed that when the Saint took possession of his Episcopal See, he found only SEVENTEEN *Christians* in the city of Neo-Cæsarea, and the adjacent country, " Les " environs, la Campagne, le pays d'alentour." (Mem. Eccles. Tom. iv. p. 677. 691. Edit. Brussells, 1706). These expressions of Tillemont, to whom I explicitly acknowledged my obligation, appeared synonymous to the word *Diocese*, the whole territory intrusted to the pastoral care of the Wonder-worker, and I added the epithet of *extensive*; because I was apprised that Neo-Cæsarea was the capital of the Polemoniac Pontus, and that the whole kingdom of Pontus, which stretched above five hundred miles along the coast of the Euxine, was divided between sixteen or seventeen Bishops. (See the Geographia Ecclesiastica of Charles de St. Paul, and Lucas Holstenius, TILLEMONT.

[3] Gibbon, p. 605. N. 156.

p. 249, 250, 251.) Thus far I may not be thought to have deſerved any cenſure; but the omiſſion of the ſubſequent part of the ſame paſſage, which imports that at his death the Wonder-worker left no more than *ſeventeen Pagans*, may ſeem to wear a partial and ſuſpicious aſpect.

Let me therefore firſt obſerve, as ſome evidence of an impartial diſpoſition, that I *eaſily* admitted, as the cool obſervation of the philoſophic Lucian, the angry and intereſted complaint of the falſe prophet Alexander, that Pontus was filled with Chriſtians. This complaint was made under the reigns of Marcus or of Commodus, with whom the impoſtor ſo admirably expoſed by Lucian was contemporary: and I had contented myſelf with remarking, that the numbers of Chriſtians muſt have been very unequally diſtributed in the ſeveral parts of Pontus, ſince the dioceſe of Neo-Cæſarea contained, above ſixty years afterwards, only ſeventeen Chriſtians. Such was the inconſiderable flock which Gregory began to feed about the year two hundred and forty, and the real or fabulous converſions aſcribed to that Wonder-working Biſhop during a reign of thirty years, are totally foreign to the ſtate of Chriſtianity in the preceding century. This obvious reflection may ſerve to anſwer the

the objection of Mr. Davis[4], and of another adversary[5], who on this occasion is more liberal than Mr. Davis of those harsh epithets so familiar to the tribe of Polemics.

XVI.

" Mr. Gibbon says[6], " Pliny was sent into " Bithynia (according to Pagi) in the year " 110." PAGI.

" Now that accurate Chronologer places it " in the year 102. See the fact *recorded* in his " Critica-Historico-Chronologica in Annales " C. Baronii, A. D. 102. p. 99. sæc. ii. " § 3."

" I appeal to my reader, Whether this " anachronism does not plainly prove that " our Historian never looked into Pagi's " Chronology, though he has not hesitated to " make a pompous reference to him in his " note[7]?"

I cannot help observing, that either Mr. Davis's Dictionary is extremely confined, or that in his Philosophy all sins are of equal magnitude. Every error of fact or language, every instance where he does not know to re-

[4] Davis, p. 136, 137.

[5] Dr. Randolph, in Chelsum's Remarks, p. 159, 160.

[6] Gibbon, p. 605. N. 157.

[7] Davis, p. 140.

concile the original and the reference, he expresses by the gentle word of *misrepresentation*. An inaccurate appeal to the sentiment of Pagi, on a subject where I must have been perfectly disinterested, might have been styled a lapse of memory, instead of being censured as the effect of vanity and ignorance. Pagi is neither a difficult nor an uncommon writer, nor could I hope to derive much additional fame from a *pompous* quotation of his writings, which I had never seen.

The words employed by Mr. Davis, of *fact*, of *record*, of *anachronism*, are unskilfully chosen, and so unhappily applied, as to betray a very shameful ignorance, either of the English language, or of the nature of this Chronological Question. The date of Pliny's government of Bithynia is not a fact recorded by any ancient writer, but an opinion which modern critics have variously formed, from the consideration of presumptive and collateral evidence. Cardinal Baronius placed the consulship of Pliny one year too late; and, as he was persuaded that the old practice of the republic still subsisted, he naturally supposed that Pliny obtained his province immediately after the expiration of his consulship. He therefore sends him into Bithynia in the year which, according to his erroneous computation, coincided

incided with the year one hundred and four (Baron. Annal. Ecclef. A. D. 103. N° 1. 104. N° 1), or, according to the true chronology, with the year one hundred and two, of the Chriftian Æra. This miftake of Baronius, Pagi, with the affiftance of his friend Cardinal Noris, undertakes to correct. From an accurate parallel of the Annals of Trajan and the Epiftles of Pliny, he deduces his proofs that Pliny remained at Rome feveral years after his Confulfhip; by his own ingenious, though fometimes fanciful theory, of the imperial Quinquennalia, &c. Pagi at laft difcovers that Pliny made his entrance into Bithynia in the year one hundred and ten. "Plinius igitur anno Chrifti CENTESIMO DECIMO Bithyniam intravit." Pagi, tom. i. p. 100.

I will be more indulgent to my adverfary than he has been to me: I will admit, that he has *looked into Pagi*; but I muft add, that he has only looked into that accurate Chronologer. To rectify the errors, which, in the courfe of a laborious and original work, had efcaped the diligence of the Cardinal, was the arduous tafk which Pagi propofed to execute: and for the fake of perfpicuity, he diftributes his criticifms acccording to the particular dates, whether juft or faulty, of the Chronology of Baronius himfelf.

ſelf. Under the year 102, Mr. Davis confuſedly ſaw a long argument about Pliny and Bithynia, and without condeſcending to read the Author whom he *pompouſly* quotes, this haſty Critic imputes to him the opinion which he had ſo laboriouſly deſtroyed.

My readers, if any readers have accompanied me thus far, muſt be ſatisfied, and indeed ſatiated, with the repeated proofs which I have made of the weight and temper of my adverſary's weapons. They have, in every aſſault, fallen dead and lifeleſs to the ground: they have more than once recoiled, and dangerouſly wounded the unſkilful hand that had preſumed to uſe them. I have now examined all the *miſrepreſentations* and *inaccuracies*, which even for a moment could perplex the ignorant, or deceive the credulous: the *few* imputations which I have neglected, are ſtill more palpably falſe, or ſtill more evidently trifling, and even the friends of Mr. Davis will ſcarcely continue to aſcribe my contempt to my fear.

PLAGIARISMS. The firſt part of his Critical Volume might admit, though it did not deſerve, a particular reply. But the eaſy, though tedious compilation, which fills the remainder[a], and which Mr. Davis has produced as the evidence of my ſhameful *plagiariſms*, may be ſet in its true

[a] Davis, p. 168—274.

light

light by three or four short and general reflexions.

I. Mr. Davis has disposed, in two columns, the passages which he thinks proper to select from my Two last Chapters, and the corresponding passages from Middleton, Barbeyrac, Beausobre, Dodwell, &c., to the most important of which he had been regularly guided by my own quotations. According to the opinion which he has conceived of literary property, to *agree* is to *follow*, and to *follow* is to *steal*. He celebrates his own sagacity with loud and reiterated applause, and declares with infinite facetiousness, that if he restored to every author the passages which Mr. Gibbon has purloined, *he* would appear as naked as the proud and gaudy Daw in the Fable, when each bird had plucked away its own plumes. Instead of being angry with Mr. Davis for the parallel which he has extended to so great a length, I am under some obligation to his industry for the copious proofs which he has furnished the reader, that my representation of some of the most important facts of Ecclesiastical Antiquity, is supported by the authority or opinion of the most ingenious and learned of the modern writers. The Public may not, perhaps, be very eager to assist Mr. Davis in his favourite amusement of *depluming* me.

They

They may think, that if the materials which compoſe my Two laſt Chapters are curious and valuable, it is of little moment to whom they properly belong. If my readers are ſatisfied with the form, the colours, the new arrangement which I have given to the labours of my predeceſſors, they may perhaps conſider me not as a contemptible Thief, but as an honeſt and induſtrious Manufacturer, who has fairly procured the raw materials, and worked them up with a laudable degree of ſkill and ſucceſs.

II. About two hundred years ago, the Court of Rome diſcovered that the ſyſtem which had been erected by ignorance muſt be defended and countenanced by the aid, or at leaſt by the abuſe, of ſcience. The groſſer legends of the middle ages were abandoned to contempt, but the ſupremacy and infallibility of two hundred Popes, the virtues of many thouſand Saints, and the miracles which they either performed or related, have been laboriouſly conſecrated in the Eccleſiaſtical Annals of Cardinal Baronius. A Theological Barometer might be formed, of which the Cardinal and our countryman Dr. Middleton ſhould conſtitute the oppoſite and remote extremities, as the former ſunk to the loweſt degree of credulity, which was compatible with learning, and the latter roſe to the higheſt pitch of ſcepticiſm, in any wiſe conſiſtent with Religion. The intermediate gradations would be filled by a line of eccleſiaſtical critics, whoſe rank has been fixed by the circumſtances of their temper and ſtudies, as well as by the ſpirit of the church or ſociety to which they were attached. It would be amuſing enough to calculate the weight of prejudice in the air of Rome, of Oxford, of Paris, and of Holland; and ſometimes to obſerve the irregular tendency of Papiſts towards freedom, ſometimes to remark the unnatural gravitation of Proteſtants towards ſlavery. But it is uſeful to borrow the aſſiſtance of ſo many learned and ingenious men, who have viewed the firſt ages of the church in every light, and from every ſituation. If we ſkilfully combine the paſſions and prejudices, the hoſtile motives and intentions, of the ſeveral theologians, we may frequently extract knowledge from credulity, moderation from zeal, and impartial truth from the moſt diſingenuous controverſy. It is the right, it is the duty of a critical hiſtorian to collect, to weigh, to ſelect the opinions of his predeceſſors; and the more diligence he has exerted in the ſearch, the more rationally he may hope to add ſome improvement to the ſtock of knowledge, the uſe of which has been common to all.

III. Besides the ideas which may be suggested by the study of the most learned and ingenious of the moderns, the historian may be indebted to them for the occasional communication of some passages of the ancients, which might otherwise have escaped his knowledge or his memory. In the consideration of any extensive subject, none will pretend to have read all that has been written, or to recollect all that they have read: nor is there any disgrace in recurring to the writers who have professedly treated any questions, which, in the course of a long narrative, we are called upon to mention in a slight and incidental manner. If I touch upon the obscure and fanciful theology of the Gnostics, I can accept without a blush the assistance of the candid Beausobre; and when, amidst the fury of contending parties, I trace the progress of ecclesiastical dominion, I am not ashamed to confess myself the grateful disciple of the impartial Mosheim. In the next Volume of my History, the Reader and the Critic must prepare themselves to see me make a still more liberal use of the labours of those indefatigable workmen who have dug deep into the mine of antiquity. The Fathers of the fourth and fifth centuries are far more voluminous than their predecessors; the writings of Jerom, of Augustin, of Chrysostom, *&c.*

cover the walls of our libraries. The ſmalleſt part is of the hiſtorical kind : yet the treatiſes which ſeem the leaſt to invite the curioſity of the reader, frequently conceal very uſeful hints, or very valuable facts. The polemic, who involves himſelf and his antagoniſts in a cloud of argumentation, ſometimes relates the origin and progreſs of the hereſy which he confutes; and the preacher who declaims againſt the luxury, deſcribes the manners, of the age; and ſeaſonably introduces the mention of ſome public calamity, that he may aſcribe it to the juſtice of offended Heaven. It would ſurely be unreaſonable to expect that the hiſtorian ſhould peruſe enormous volumes, with the uncertain hope of extracting a few intereſting lines, or that he ſhould ſacrifice whole days to the momentary amuſement of his Reader. Fortunately for us both, the diligence of eccleſiaſtical critics has facilitated our inquiries: the compilations of Tillemont might alone be conſidered as an immenſe repertory of truth and fable, of almoſt all that the Fathers have preſerved, or invented, or believed; and if we equally avail ourſelves of the labours of contending ſectaries, we ſhall often diſcover, that the ſame paſſages which the prudence of one of the diſputants would have ſuppreſſed or diſguiſed, are placed in the moſt conſpicuous

 light

light by the active and interested zeal of his adversary. On these occasions, what is the duty of a faithful historian, who derives from some modern writer the knowledge of some ancient testimony, which he is desirous of introducing into his own narrative? It is his duty, and it has been my invariable practice, to consult the original; to study with attention the words, the design, the spirit, the context, the situation of the passage to which I had been referred; and before I appropriated it to my own use, to justify my own declaration, "that I had carefully examined all the original materials that could illustrate the subject "which I had undertaken to treat." If this important obligation has sometimes been imperfectly fulfilled, I have only omitted what it would have been impracticable for me to perform. The greatest city in the world is still destitute of that useful institution, a public library; and the writer who has undertaken to treat any large historical subject, is reduced to the necessity of purchasing, for his private use, a numerous and valuable collection of the books which must form the basis of his work. The diligence of his booksellers will not always prove successful; and the candour of his readers will not *always* expect, that, for the sake of verifying an accidental quotation of ten lines, he should

ſhould load himſelf with an uſeleſs and expenſive ſeries of ten volumes. In a very few inſtances, where I had not the opportunity of conſulting the originals, I have adopted their teſtimony on the faith of modern guides, of whoſe fidelity I was ſatisfied; but on theſe occaſions [9], inſtead of decking myſelf with the borrowed plumes of Tillemont or Lardner, I have been moſt ſcrupulouſly exact in marking the extent of my reading, and the ſource of my information. This diſtinction, which a ſenſe of truth and modeſty had engaged me to expreſs, is ungenerouſly abuſed by Mr. Davis, who ſeems happy to inform his readers, that "in ONE inſtance (Chap. xvi. 164. or, in the "firſt edition, 163.) I have, by an unaccount-"able overſight, unfortunately for myſelf, for-"got to drop the modern, and that I modeſtly "diſclaim all knowledge of Athanaſius, but what "I had picked up from Tillemont [1]." Without animadverting on the decency of theſe expreſſions, which are now grown familiar to me, I ſhall content myſelf with obſerving, that as I had frequently quoted Euſebius, or Cyprian, or Tertullian, *becauſe* I had read them; ſo, in this inſtance, I only made my reference to Tillemont,

[9] Gibbon, p. 605, N. 156; p. 606, N. 161; p. 690, N. 164; p. 699, N. 178.

[1] Davis, p. 273.

lemont, *because* I had not read, and did not possess, the works of Athanasius. The progress of my undertaking has since directed me to peruse the Historical Apologies of the Archbishop of Alexandria, whose life is a very interesting part of the age in which he lived; and if Mr. Davis should have the curiosity to look into my Second Volume, he will find that I make a free and frequent appeal to the writings of Athanasius. Whatever may be the opinion or practice of my adversary, this I apprehend to be the dealing of a fair and honourable man.

IV. The historical monuments of the three first centuries of ecclesiastical antiquity are neither very numerous, nor very prolix. From the end of the Acts of the Apostles, to the time when the first Apology of Justin Martyr was presented, there intervened a dark and doubtful period of fourscore years; and, even if the Epistles of Ignatius should be approved by the critic, they could not be very serviceable to the historian. From the middle of the second, to the beginning of the fourth, century, we gain our knowledge of the state and progress of Christianity from the successive Apologies which were occasionally composed by Justin, Athenagoras, Tertullian, Origen, *&c.*; from the Epistles of Cyprian; from a few *sincere* acts of of the Martyrs; from some moral or controversial tracts, which indirectly explain the events and manners of the times; from the rare and accidental notice which profane writers have taken of the Christian sect; from the declamatory Narrative which celebrates the deaths of the persecutors; and from the Ecclesiastical History of Eusebius, who has preserved some valuable fragments of more early writers. Since the revival of letters, these original materials have been the common fund of critics and historians: nor has it ever been imagined, that the absolute and exclusive property of a passage in Eusebius or Tertullian was acquired by the first who had an opportunity of quoting it. The learned work of Mosheim, *de Rebus Christianis ante Constantinum*, was printed in the year 1753; and if I were possessed of the patience and disingenuity of Mr. Davis, I would engage to find all the ancient testimonies that he has alleged, in the writings of Dodwell or Tillemont, which were published before the end of the last century. But if I were animated by any malevolent intentions against Dodwell or Tillemont, I could as easily, and as unfairly, fix on *them* the guilt of Plagiarism, by producing the same passages transcribed or translated at full length in the Annals of Cardinal Baronius. Let not criticism be any longer disgraced

graced by the practice of such unworthy arts. Instead of admitting suspicions as false as they are ungenerous, candour will acknowledge, that Mosheim or Dodwell, Tillemont or Baronius, enjoyed the same right, and often were under the same obligation, of quoting the passages which they had read, and which were indispensably requisite to confirm the truth and substance of their similar narratives. Mr. Davis is so far from allowing me the benefit of this common indulgence, or rather of this common right, that he stigmatizes with the name of *Plagiarism* a close and literal agreement with Dodwell in the account of some parts of the persecution of Diocletian, where a few chapters of Eusebius and Lactantius, perhaps of Lactantius alone, are the sole materials from whence our knowledge could be derived, and where, if I had not transcribed, I must have invented. He is even bold enough (*bold* is not the *proper* word) to conceive some hopes of persuading his readers that an Historian who has employed several years of his life, and several hundred pages, on the Decline and Fall of the Roman Empire, had never read Orosius, or the Augustan History; and that he was forced to borrow, at second-hand, his quotations from the Theodosian Code. I cannot profess myself very desirous of Mr. Davis's acquaintance;

quaintance; but if he will take the trouble of calling at my houſe any afternoon when I am *not* at home, my ſervant ſhall ſhew him my library, which he will find tolerably well furniſhed with the uſeful authors, ancient as well as modern, eccleſiaſtical as well as profane, who have *directly* ſupplied me with the materials of my Hiſtory.

The peculiar reaſons, and they are not of the moſt flattering kind, which urged me to repel the furious and feeble attack of Mr. Davis, have been already mentioned. But ſince I am drawn thus reluctantly into the liſts of controverſy, I ſhall not retire till I have ſaluted, either with ſtern defiance or gentle courteſy, the theological champions who have ſignalized their ardour to break a lance againſt the ſhield of a *Pagan* adverſary. The Fifteenth and Sixteenth Chapters have been honoured with the notice of ſeveral writers, whoſe names and characters ſeemed to promiſe more maturity of judgment and learning than could reaſonably be expected from the unfiniſhed ſtudies of a Batchelor of Arts. The Reverend Mr. Apthorpe, Dr. Watſon, the Regius Profeſſor of Divinity in the Univerſity of Cambridge, Dr. Chelſum of Chriſt Church, and his aſſociate Dr. Randolph, Preſident of Corpus Chriſti

College, and the Lady Margaret's Profeſſor of Divinity in the Univerſity of Oxford, have given me a fair right, which, however, I ſhall not abuſe, of freely declaring my opinion on the ſubject of their reſpective criticiſms.

MR. APTHORPE.

If I am not miſtaken, Mr. Apthorpe was the firſt who announced to the Public his intention of examining the intereſting ſubject which I had treated in the Two laſt Chapters of my Hiſtory. The multitude of collateral and acceſſary ideas which preſented themſelves to the Author, inſenſibly ſwelled the bulk of his papers to the ſize of a large volume in octavo; the publication was delayed many months beyond the time of the firſt advertiſement; and when Mr. Apthorpe's Letters appeared, I was ſurpriſed to find, that I had *ſcarcely* any intereſt or concern in their contents. They are filled with general obſervations on the Study of Hiſtory, with a large and uſeful catalogue of Hiſtorians, and with a variety of reflections, moral and religious, all preparatory to the direct and formal conſideration of my Two laſt Chapters, which Mr. Apthorpe ſeems to reſerve for the ſubject of a Second Volume. I ſincerely reſpect the learning, the piety, and the candour of this Gentleman, and muſt conſider it as a mark of his eſteem, that he has thought proper to begin his approaches at ſo

great

great a diſtance from the fortifications which he deſigned to attack.

When Dr. Watſon gave to the Public his Apology for Chriſtianity, in a Series of Letters, he addreſſed them to the Author of the Decline and Fall of the Roman Empire, with a juſt confidence that he had conſidered this important object in a manner not unworthy of his antagoniſt or of himſelf. Dr. Watſon's mode of thinking bears a liberal and philoſophic caſt; his thoughts are expreſſed with ſpirit, and that ſpirit is always tempered by politeneſs and moderation. Such is the man whom I ſhould be happy to call my friend, and whom I ſhould not bluſh to call my antagoniſt. But the ſame motives which might tempt me to accept, or even to ſolicit, a private and amicable conference, diſſuaded me from entering into a public controverſy with a Writer of ſo reſpectable a character; and I embraced the earlieſt opportunity of expreſſing to Dr. Watſon himſelf, how ſincerely I agreed with him in thinking, "That as the world is "now poſſeſſed of the opinion of us both upon "the ſubject in queſtion, it may be perhaps "as proper for us both to leave it in this "ſtate[2]." The nature of the ingenious Pro- DR. WATSON.

[2] Watſon's Apology for Chriſtianity, p. 200.

fessor's Apology contributed to strengthen the insuperable reluctance to engage in hostile altercation which was common to us both, by convincing me, that such an altercation was unnecessary as well as unpleasant. He very justly and politely declares, that a considerable part, near seventy pages, of his small volume are not directed to me[3], but to a set of men whom he places in an odious and contemptible light. He leaves to other hands the defence of the leading Ecclesiastics, even of the primitive church; and without being *very* anxious, either to soften their vices and indiscretion, or to aggravate the cruelty of the Heathen Persecutors, he passes over in silence the greatest part of my Sixteenth Chapter. It is not so much the purpose of the Apologist to examine the facts which have been advanced by the Historian, as to remove the impressions which may have been formed by many of his Readers; and the remarks of Dr. Watson consist more properly of general argumentation than of particular criticism. He fairly owns, that I have expressly allowed the full and irresistible weight of the *first* great cause of the success of Christianity[4], and he is too candid to deny

[3] Watson's Apology for Christianity, p. 202—268.
[4] Id. p. 5.

that

that the five *secondary* causes, which I had attempted to explain, operated with *some* degree of active energy towards the accomplishment of that great event. The only question which remains between us, relates to the *degree* of the weight and effect of those secondary causes; and as I am persuaded that our philosophy is not of the dogmatic kind, we should soon acknowledge that this precise degree cannot be ascertained by reasoning, nor perhaps be expressed by words. In the course of this inquiry, some incidental difficulties have arisen, which I had stated with impartiality, and which Dr. Watson resolves with ingenuity and temper. If in some instances he seems to have misapprehended my sentiments, I may hesitate whether I should impute the fault to my own want of clearness or to his want of attention, but I can never entertain a suspicion that Dr. Watson would descend to employ the disingenuous arts of vulgar controversy.

There is, however, one passage, and one passage only, which must not pass without some explanation; and I shall the more eagerly embrace this occasion to illustrate what I had said, as the misconstruction of my true meaning seems to have made an involuntary, but unfavourable, impression on the liberal mind of Dr. Watson. As I endeavour *not* to palliate the severity,

ſeverity, but to diſcover the motives, of the Roman Magiſtrates, I had remarked, "it "was in vain that the oppreſſed Believer "aſſerted the unalienable rights of con-"ſcience and private judgment. Though his "ſituation might excite the pity, his argu-"ments could never reach the underſtanding, "either of the philoſophic or of the believing "part of the Pagan world[5]." The humanity of Dr. Watſon takes fire on the ſuppoſed provocation, and he aſks me with unuſual quickneſs, "How, Sir, are the arguments for liberty "of conſcience ſo exceedingly inconcluſive, "that you think them incapable of reaching "the underſtanding even of philoſophers[6]?" He continues to obſerve, that a captious adverſary would embrace with avidity the opportunity this paſſage *affords*, of blotting my character with the odious ſtain of being a Perſecutor; a ſtain which no learning can wipe out, which no genius or ability can render amiable; and though he himſelf does not entertain ſuch an opinion of my principles, his ingenuity tries in vain to provide me with the means of eſcape.

I muſt lament that I have not been ſucceſſful in the explanation of a very ſimple notion

[5] Gibbon, p. 625. [6] Watſon, p. 185.

of the ſpirit both of philoſophy and of polytheiſm, which I have repeatedly inculcated. The arguments which aſſert the rights of conſcience are not inconcluſive in themſelves, but the underſtanding of the Greeks and Romans was fortified againſt their evidence by an invincible prejudice. When we liſten to the voice of Bayle, of Locke, and of genuine reaſon, in favour of religious toleration, we ſhall eaſily perceive that our moſt forcible appeal is made to our mutual feelings. If the Jew were allowed to argue with the Inquiſitor, he would requeſt that for a moment they might exchange their different ſituations, and might ſafely aſk his Catholic Tyrant, whether the fear of death would compel *him* to enter the ſynagogue, to receive the mark of circumciſion, and to partake of the paſchal lamb. As ſoon as the caſe of perſecution was brought home to the breaſt of the Inquiſitor, he muſt have found ſome difficulty in ſuppreſſing the dictates of natural equity, which would inſinuate to his conſcience, that he could have no right to inflict thoſe puniſhments which, under ſimilar circumſtances, he would eſteem it as his duty to encounter. But this argument could not reach the underſtanding of a Polytheiſt, or of an ancient Philoſopher. The former was ready, whenever he was ſummoned, or indeed with-

out

out being ſummoned, to fall proſtrate before the altars of any Gods who were adored in any part of the world, and to admit a vague perſuaſion of the *truth* and divinity of the moſt different modes of religion. The Philoſopher, who conſidered them, at leaſt in their literal ſenſe, as equally *falſe* and abſurd, was not aſhamed to diſguiſe his ſentiments, and to frame his actions according to the laws of his country, which impoſed the ſame obligation on the Philoſophers and the people. When Pliny declared, that whatever was the opinion of the Chriſtians, their obſtinacy deſerved puniſhment, the abſurd cruelty of Pliny was excuſed in his own eye, by the conſciouſneſs that, in the ſituation of the Chriſtians, he would not have refuſed the religious compliance which he exacted. I ſhall not repeat, that the Pagan worſhip was a matter, not of *opinion*, but of *cuſtom*; that the toleration of the Romans was confined to nations or families who followed the practice of their anceſtors; and that in the firſt ages of Chriſtianity their perſecution of the individuals who departed from the eſtabliſhed religion was neither moderated by pure reaſon, nor inflamed by excluſive zeal. But I only deſire to appeal, from the haſty apprehenſion, to the more deliberate judgment, of Dr. Watſon himſelf. Should there ſtill remain any difference of opinion between us, I shall be satisfied, if he will consider me as a sincere, though perhaps unsuccessful, lover of truth, and as a firm friend to civil and ecclesiastical freedom.

Dr. Chelsum and Dr. Randolph.

Far be it from me, or from any faithful Historian, to impute to respectable societies the faults of some individual members. Our two Universities most undoubtedly contain the same mixture, and most probably the same proportions, of zeal and moderation, of reason and superstition. Yet there is much less difference between the smoothness of the Ionic, and the roughness of the Doric dialect, than may be found between the polished style of Dr. Watson, and the coarse language of Mr. Davis, Dr. Chelsum, or Dr. Randolph. The second of these Critics, Dr. Chelsum of Christ Church, is unwilling that the world should forget that *he* was the first who sounded to arms, that *he* was the first who furnished the antidote to the poison, and who, as early as the month of October of the year 1776, published his *Strictures* on the Two last Chapters of Mr. Gibbon's History. The success of a pamphlet, which he modestly styles imperfect and ill-digested, encouraged him to resume the controversy. In the beginning of the present year, his Remarks made their second appearance, with some alteration of form, and a large increaſe of bulk; and the author who ſeems to fight under the protection of two epiſcopal banners, has prefixed, in the front of his volume, his name and titles, which in the former edition he had leſs honourably ſuppreſſed. His confidence is fortified by the alliance and communications of a *diſtinguiſhed* Writer, Dr. Randolph, *&c.* who, on a proper occaſion, would, no doubt, be ready to bear as honourable teſtimony to the merit and reputation of Dr. Chelſum. The two friends are indeed ſo happily united by art and nature, that if the author of the Remarks had not pointed out the valuable communications of the Margaret Profeſſor, it would have been impoſſible to ſeparate their reſpective property. Writers who poſſeſs any freedom of mind, may be known from each other by the peculiar character of their ſtyle and ſentiments; but the champions who are inliſted in the ſervice of Authority, commonly wear the uniform of the regiment. Oppreſſed with the ſame yoke, covered with the ſame trappings, they heavily move along, perhaps not with an equal pace, in the ſame beaten track of prejudice and preferment. Yet I ſhould expoſe my own injuſtice, were I abſolutely to confound with Mr. Davis the two Doctors in Divinity, who are joined in one volume. The three Critics appear

appear to be animated by the same implacable resentment against the Historian of the Roman Empire; they are alike disposed to support the same opinions by the same arts; and if in the language of the two latter, the disregard of politeness is somewhat less gross and indecent, the difference is not of such a magnitude as to excite in my breast any lively sensations of gratitude. It was the misfortune of Mr. Davis that he undertook to *write* before he had *read*. He set out with the stock of authorities which he found in my quotations, and boldly ventured to play his reputation against mine. Perhaps he may now repent of a loss which is not easily recovered; but if I had not surmounted my almost insuperable reluctance to a public dispute, many a reader might still be dazzled by the vehemence of his affertions, and might still believe that Mr. Davis had detected several wilful and important misrepresentations in my Two last Chapters. But the confederate Doctors appear to be scholars of a higher form and longer experience; they enjoy a certain rank in their academical world; and as their zeal is enlightened by some rays of knowledge, so their desire to ruin the credit of their adversary is occasionally checked by the apprehension of injuring their own. These restraints, to which Mr. Davis was a stranger, have confined them to a very narrow and humble path of hiſtorical criticiſm; and if I were to correct, according to their wiſhes, all the particular facts againſt which they have advanced any objections, theſe corrections, admitted in their fulleſt extent, would hardly furniſh materials for a decent liſt of *errata*.

The *dogmatical* part of their work, which in every ſenſe of the word deſerves that appellation, is ill adapted to engage my attention. I had declined the conſideration of theological arguments, when they were managed by a candid and liberal adverſary; and it would be inconſiſtent enough, if I ſhould have refuſed to draw my ſword in honourable combat againſt the keen and well-tempered weapon of Dr. Watſon, for the ſole purpoſe of encountering the ruſtic cudgel of two ſtaunch and ſturdy Polemics.

I ſhall not enter any farther into the character and conduct of Cyprian, as I am ſenſible that, if the opinion of Le Clerc, Moſheim, and myſelf, is reprobated by Dr. Chelſum and his ally, the difference muſt ſubſiſt, till we ſhall entertain the ſame notions of moral virtue and eccleſiaſtical power[7]. If Dr. Randolph will allow that the primitive Clergy received,

[7] Gibbon, p. 558, 559. Chelſum, p. 132—139.

managed, and distributed the tythes, and other charitable donations of the faithful, the dispute between *us*, will be a dispute of words[8]. I shall not amuse myself with proving that the learned Origen must have derived from the *inspired* authority of the Church his knowledge, not indeed of the *authenticity*, but of the *inspiration* of the *four* Evangelists, *two* of whom are not in the rank of the Apostles[9]. I shall submit to the judgment of the Public, whether the Athanasian Creed is not read and received in the Church of England, and whether the wisest and most virtuous of the Pagans[1] believed the Catholic faith, which is declared in the Athanasian Creed to be absolutely necessary for salvation. As little shall I think myself interested in the elaborate disquisitions with which the Author of the Remarks has filled a great number of pages, concerning the famous testimony of Josephus, the passages of Irenæus and Theophilus, which relate to the gift of miracles, and the origin of circumcision in Palestine or in Egypt[2]. If I have rejected, and rejected with some contempt, the *interpolation* which pious fraud has very aukwardly inserted in the text

[8] Gibbon, p. 592. Randolph in Chelsum, p. 122.
[9] Gibbon, p. 551, Note 33. Chelsum, p. 39.
[1] Gibbon, p. 565, Note 70. Chelsum, p. 66.
[2] Chelsum's Remarks, p. 13—19. 67—91. 180—185.

of

of Josephus, I may deem myself secure behind the shield of learned and pious critics (See in particular Le Clerc, in his Ars Critica, part iii. sect. i. c. 15. and Lardner's Testimonies, Vol. i. p. 150, &c.), who have condemned this passage: and I think it very natural that Dr. Chelsum should embrace the contrary opinion, which is not destitute of able advocates. The passages of Irenæus and Theophilus were thoroughly sifted in the controversy about the duration of Miracles; and as the Works of Dr. Middleton may be found in every library, so it is not impossible that a diligent search may still discover some remains of the writings of his adversaries. In mentioning the confession of the Syrians of Palestine, that they had received from Egypt the rite of circumcision, I had simply alleged the testimony of Herodotus, without expressly adopting the sentiment of Marsham. But I had always imagined, that in these doubtful and indifferent questions, which have been solemnly argued before the tribunal of the Public, every scholar was at liberty to chuse his side, without assigning his reasons; nor can I yet persuade myself, that either Dr. Chelsum, or myself, are likely to enforce, by any new arguments, the opinions which we have respectively followed. The only novelty for which I can perceive myself indebted to Dr. Chelsum, is the

the very extraordinary Scepticism which he insinuates concerning the time of Herodotus, who, according to the chronology of some, flourished during the time of the Jewish captivity [a]. Can it be necessary to inform a Divine, that the captivity which lasted seventy years, according to the prophecy of Jeremiah, was terminated in the year 536 before Christ, by the edict which Cyrus published in the first year of his reign (Jeremiah, xxv. 11, 12. xxix. 10. Ezra, i. 1. &c. Usher and Prideaux, under the years 606 and 536.)? Can it be necessary to inform a man of letters, that Herodotus was fifty-three years old at the commencement of the Peloponnesian war (Aulus Gellius, Noct. Attic. xv. 23. from the commentaries of Pamphila), and consequently that he was born in the year before Christ 484, fifty-two years after the end of the Jewish captivity? As this well attested fact is not exposed to the slightest doubt or difficulty, I am somewhat curious to learn the names of those unknown authors, whose chronology Dr. Chelsum has allowed as the specious foundation of a probable hypothesis. The Author of the Remarks does not seem indeed to have cultivated, with much care or success, the province of literary history; as

[a] Chelsum, p. 15.

a very

a very moderate acquaintance with that uſeful branch of knowledge would have ſaved him from a poſitive miſtake, much leſs excuſable than the doubt which he entertains about the time of Herodotus. He ſtyles Suidas "a "*Heathen* writer, who lived about the end of "the *tenth* century [4]." I admit the period which he aſſigns to Suidas; and which is well aſcertained by Dr. Bentley (See his Reply to Boyle, p. 22, 23.). We are led to fix this epoch, by the chronology which this *Heathen* writer has deduced from Adam, to the death of the emperor John Zimiſces, A. D. 975: and a crowd of paſſages might be produced, as the unanſwerable evidence of his Chriſtianity. But the moſt unanſwerable of all is the very date, which is not diſputed between us. The philoſophers who flouriſhed under Juſtinian (See Agathias, l. ii. p. 65, 66.), appear to have been the laſt of the Heathen writers: and the ancient religion of the Greeks was annihilated almoſt four hundred years before the birth of Suidas.

After this animadverſion, which is not intended either to inſult the failings of my Adverſary, or to provide a convenient excuſe for my own errors, I ſhall proceed to ſelect *two*

[4] Chelſum, p. 73.

important

important parts of Dr. Chelſum's Remarks, from which the candid reader may form ſome opinion of the whole. They relate to the military ſervice of the firſt Chriſtians, and to the hiſtorical character of Euſebius; and I ſhall review them with the leſs reluctance, as it may not be impoſſible to pick up ſomething curious and uſeful even in the barren waſte of controverſy.

I.

MILITARY SERVICE OF THE FIRST CHRISTIANS.

In repreſenting the errors of the primitive Chriſtians, which flowed from an exceſs of virtue, I had obſerved, *that* they expoſed themſelves to the reproaches of the Pagans, by their obſtinate refuſal to take an active part in the civil adminiſtration, or military defence of the empire; *that* the objections of Celſus appear to have been mutilated by his adverſary Origen; and *that* the Apologiſts, to whom the public dangers were urged, returned obſcure and ambiguous anſwers, as they were unwilling to diſcloſe the true ground of their ſecurity, their opinion of the approaching end of the world [5]. In another place I had related, from the Acts of Ruinart, the action and puniſhment of the Centurion Marcellus, who was put to death for renouncing the ſervice in a public and ſeditious manner [6].

[5] Gibbon, p. 580, 581. [6] Id. p. 680.

On this occasion Dr. Chelsum is extremely alert. He denies my facts, controverts my opinions, and, with a politeness worthy of Mr. Davis himself, insinuates that I borrowed the story of Marcellus, not from Ruinart, but from Voltaire. My learned Adversary thinks it highly improbable that Origen should dare to *mutilate* the objections of Celsus, "whose work "was, in all probability, extant at the time he "made this reply. In such case, had he even "been inclined to treat his adversary unfairly, "he must yet surely have been with-held from "the attempt, through the fear of detec- "tion[7]." The experience both of ancient and modern controversy has indeed convinced me that this reasoning, just and natural as it may seem, is totally inconclusive, and that the generality of disputants, especially in religious contests, are of a much more daring and intrepid spirit. For the truth of this remark, I shall content myself with producing a recent and very singular example, in which Dr. Chelsum himself is personally interested. He charges[8] me with passing over in "silence the important "and unsuspected testimony of a Heathen his- "torian (Dion Cassius) to the persecution of "Domitian; and he affirms, that I have pro-

[7] Chelsum, p. 118, 119.

[8] Id. p. 188.

"duced

"duced that teſtimony ſo far only as it relates "to Clemens and Domitilla; yet in the very "ſame paſſage follows immediately, that on "a like accuſation MANY OTHERS were alſo "condemned. Some of them were put to "death, others ſuffered the confiſcation of "their goods[9]." Although I ſhould not be aſhamed to undertake the apology of Nero or Domitian, if I thought them innocent of any particular crime with which zeal or malice had unjuſtly branded their memory; yet I ſhould indeed bluſh, if, in favour of tyranny, or even in favour of virtue, I had ſuppreſſed the truth and evidence of hiſtorical facts. But the Reader will feel ſome ſurpriſe, when he has convinced himſelf that, in the three editions of my Firſt Volume, after relating the death of Clemens, and the exile of Domitilla, I continue to allege the ENTIRE TESTIMONY of Dion, in the following words: "and ſentences either "of death, or of confiſcation, were pronounced "againſt a GREAT NUMBER OF PERSONS who "were involved in the SAME accuſation. The "guilt imputed to their charge, was that of "Atheiſm and Jewiſh manners; a ſingular "aſſociation of ideas which cannot with any "propriety be applied except to the Chriſtians,

9 Gibbon, p 645.

" as they were obſcurely and imperfectly " viewed by the magiſtrates and writers of " that period." Dr. Chelſum has not been deterred, by the fear of detection, from this ſcandalous mutilation of the popular work of a living adverſary. But Celſus had been dead above fifty years before Origen publiſhed his Apology; and the copies of an ancient work, inſtead of being inſtantaneouſly multiplied by the operation of the preſs, were ſeparately and ſlowly tranſcribed by the labour of the hand.

If any modern Divine ſhould ſtill maintain that the fidelity of Origen was ſecured by motives more honourable than the fear of detection, he may learn from Jerom the difference of the *gymnaſtic* and *dogmatic* ſtyles. Truth is the object of the one, Victory of the other; and the ſame arts which would diſgrace the ſincerity of the teacher, ſerve only to diſplay the ſkill of the diſputant. After juſtifying his own practice by that of the orators and philoſophers, Jerom defends himſelf by the more reſpectable authority of Chriſtian Apologiſts. " How many thouſand lines, ſays he, have " been compoſed againſt *Celſus* and Porphyry, " by *Origen*, Methodius, Euſebius, Apollinaris? " Conſider with what arguments, with what " ſlippery problems, they elude the inventions " of the Devil; and how in their controverſy

" with

" with the Gentiles, they are ſometimes oblig-
" ed to ſpeak, not what they really think, but
" what is moſt advantageous for the cauſe they
" defend." " Origenes, &c. multis verſuum
" millibus ſcribunt adverſus Celſum et Por-
" phyrium. Conſiderate quibus argumentis et
" quam lubricis problematibus diaboli ſpiritu
" contexta ſubvertunt: et quia interdum co-
" guntur loqui, non quod ſentiunt, ſed quod
" neceſſe eſt dicunt adverſus ea quæ dicunt
" Gentiles." (Pro Libris adverſ. Jovinian. Apolog. Tom. ii. p. 135.)

Yet Dr. Chelſum may ſtill aſk, and he has a right to aſk, why in this particular inſtance I ſuſpect the pious Origen of mutilating the objections of his adverſary. From a very obvious, and, in my opinion, a very deciſive, circumſtance. Celſus was a Greek philoſopher, the friend of Lucian; and I thought that, although he might ſupport error by ſophiſtry, he would not write nonſenſe in his own language. I renounce my ſuſpicion, if the moſt attentive reader is able to underſtand the deſign and purport of a paſſage which is given as a formal quotation from Celſus, and which begins with the following words: Ου μην ουδε εκεινο ανεκτον σου λεγοντος, ως, &c. (Origen contr. Celſum, l. viii. p. 425. edit. Spencer, Cantab. 1677.) I have carefully inſpected the original, I have availed myſelf

myſelf of the learning of Spencer, and even Bouhereau (for I ſhall always diſclaim the abſurd and affected pedantry of uſing without ſcruple a Latin verſion, but of deſpiſing the aid of a French tranſlation), and the ill ſucceſs of my efforts has countenanced the ſuſpicion to which I ſtill adhere, with a juſt mixture of doubt and heſitation. Origen very boldly denies, that any of the Chriſtians have affirmed what is imputed to them by Celſus, in this unintelligible quotation; and it may eaſily be credited, that none had maintained what none can comprehend. Dr. Chelſum has produced the words of Origen; but on this occaſion there is a ſtrange ambiguity in the language of the modern Divine [1], as if he wiſhed to inſinuate what he dared not affirm; and every reader muſt conclude, from his ſtate of the queſtion, that Origen expreſsly denied the truth of the *accuſation* of Celſus, who had *accuſed* the Chriſtians of declining to aſſiſt their fellow-ſubjects in the military defence of the empire, aſſailed on every ſide by the arms of the Barbarians.

Will Dr. Chelſum juſtify to the world, can he juſtify to his own feelings, the abuſe which he has made even of the privileges of the Gymnaſtic ſtyle? Careleſs and haſty indeed muſt

[1] Chelſum, p. 118.

have

have been his peruſal of Origen, if he did not perceive that the ancient Apologiſt, who makes a ſtand on ſome incidental queſtion, admits the accuſation of his adverſary, that the Chriſtians *refuſed* to bear arms even at the command of their ſovereign. "και ου συστρατευομεθα μεν αυτῳ, καν επειγῃ." (Origen, l. viii. p. 427.) He endeavours to palliate this undutiful refuſal, by repreſenting that the Chriſtians had their peculiar camps, in which they inceſſantly combated for the ſafety of the emperor and the empire, by lifting up their right hands—in prayer. The Apologiſt ſeems to hope that his country will be ſatisfied with this ſpiritual aid, and dexterouſly confounding the colleges of Roman prieſts with the multitudes which ſwelled the Catholic Church, he claims for his brethren, in all the provinces, the exemption from military ſervice, which was enjoyed by the ſacerdotal order. But as this excuſe might not readily be allowed, Origen looks forwards with a lively faith to that auſpicious Revolution, which Celſus had rejected as impoſſible, when all the nations of the habitable earth, renouncing their paſſions and their arms, ſhould embrace the pure doctrines of the Goſpel, and lead a life of peace and innocence under the immediate protection of Heaven. The faith of Origen ſeems to be principally founded on the predictions of the Prophet Zephaniah (See iii. 9, 10.); and he prudently obſerves, that the Prophets often ſpeak ſecret things (εν αποῤῥητω λεγουσι, p. 426.), which may be underſtood by thoſe who can underſtand them; and that if this ſtupendous change cannot be effected while we retain our bodies, it may be accompliſhed as ſoon as we ſhall be releaſed from them. Such is the reaſoning of Origen: though I have not followed the order, I have faithfully preſerved the ſubſtance, of it; which fully juſtifies the truth and propriety of my obſervations.

The execution of Marcellus, the Centurion, is naturally connected with the Apology of Origen, as the former declared by his actions, what the latter had affirmed in his writings, that the conſcience of a devout Chriſtian would not allow him to bear arms, even at the command of his Sovereign. I had repreſented this religious ſcruple as *one* of the motives which provoked Marcellus, on the day of a public feſtival, to throw away the enſigns of his office; and I preſumed to obſerve, that ſuch an act of deſertion would have been puniſhed in any government according to martial or even civil law. Dr. Chelſum [a] very *bluntly*

[a] Chelſum, p. 114—117.

accuſes

accuſes me of miſrepreſenting the ſtory, and of ſuppreſſing thoſe circumſtances which would have defended the Centurion from the unjuſt imputation thrown by me upon his conduct. The diſpute between the Advocate for Marcellus and myſelf, lies in a very narrow compaſs; as the whole evidence is compriſed in a ſhort, ſimple, and, I believe, authentic narrative.

1. In another place I obſerved, and even preſſed the obſervation, "that the innumerable Deities and rites of Polytheiſm were "cloſely interwoven with every circumſtance "of buſineſs or pleaſure, of public or of private "life;" and I had particularly ſpecified how much the Roman diſcipline was connected with the national ſuperſtition. A ſolemn oath of fidelity was repeated every year in the name of the Gods and of the genius of the Emperor, public and daily ſacrifices were performed at the head of the camp, the legionary was continually tempted, or rather compelled, to join in the idolatrous worſhip of his fellow-ſoldiers, and had not any ſcruples been entertained of the lawfulneſs of war, it is not eaſy to underſtand how any ſerious Chriſtian could inliſt under a banner which has been juſtly termed the *rival of the Croſs.* "Vexilla æmula Chriſti." (Tertullian de Corona Militis, c. xi.) With regard to the ſoldiers, who before their converſion

were already engaged in the military life, fear, habit, ignorance, neceſſity might bend them to ſome acts of occaſional conformity; and as long as they abſtained from abſolute and intentional idolatry, their behaviour was excuſed by the indulgent, and cenſured by the more rigid caſuiſts. (See the whole Treatiſe *De Corona Militis.*) We are ignorant of the adventures and character of the Centurion Marcellus, how long he had conciliated the profeſſion of arms and of the Goſpel, whether he was only a Catechumen, or whether he was initiated by the Sacrament of Baptiſm. We are likewiſe at a loſs to aſcertain the particular act of idolatry which ſo ſuddenly and ſo forcibly provoked his pious indignation. As he declared his faith in the midſt of a public entertainment given on the birth-day of Galerius, he muſt have been ſtartled by ſome of the ſacred and convivial rites (Convivia iſta profana reputans) of prayers, or vows, or libations, or, perhaps, by the offenſive circumſtance of eating the meats which had been offered to the idols. But the ſcruples of Marcellus were not confined to theſe accidental impurities; they evidently reached the eſſential duties of his profeſſion; and when before the tribunal of the magiſtrates, he avowed his faith at the hazard of his life, the Centurion declared, as his cool and determined perſuaſion, that it does not

become

become a Christian man, who is the soldier of the Lord Christ, to bear arms for any object of earthly concern. "Non enim decebat "Christianum hominem molestiis secularibus "militare, qui Christo Domino militat." A formal declaration, which clearly disengages from each other the different questions of war and idolatry. With regard to both these questions, as they were understood by the primitive Christians, I wish to refer the Reader to the sentiments and authorities of Mr. Moyle, a bold and ingenious critic, who read the Fathers as their judge, and not as their slave, and who has refuted, with the most patient candour, all that learned prejudice could suggest in favour of the silly story of the Thundering Legion. (See Moyle's Works, Vol. ii. p. 84—88. 111—116. 163—212. 298—302. 327—341.) And here let me add, that the passage of Origen, who in the name of his brethren disclaims the duty of military service, is understood by Mr. Moyle in its true and obvious signification.

2. I know not where Dr. Chelsum has imbibed the principles of logic or morality which teach him to approve the conduct of Marcellus, who threw down his rod, his belt, and his arms, at the head of the legion, and publicly renounced the military service, *at the very time* when he found himself obliged to offer sa-

 crifice.

crifice. Yet ſurely this is a very falſe notion of the condition and duties of a Roman Centurion. Marcellus was bound, by a ſolemn oath, to ſerve with fidelity till he ſhould be regularly diſcharged; and according to the ſentiments which Dr. Chelſum aſcribes to him, he was not releaſed from his oath by any miſtaken opinion of the unlawfulneſs of war. I would propoſe it as a caſe of conſcience to any philoſopher, or even to any caſuiſt in Europe, Whether a particular order, which cannot be reconciled with virtue or piety, diſſolves the ties of a general and lawful obligation? And whether, if they had been conſulted by the Chriſtian Centurion, they would not have directed him to increaſe his diligence in the execution of his military functions, to refuſe to yield to any act of idolatry, and patiently to expect the conſequences of ſuch a refuſal? But, inſtead of obeying the mild and moderate dictates of religion, inſtead of diſtinguiſhing between the duties of the ſoldier and of the Chriſtian, Marcellus, with imprudent zeal, ruſhed forwards to ſeize the crown of martyrdom. He might have privately confeſſed himſelf guilty to the tribune or præfect under whom he ſerved: he choſe on the day of a public feſtival to diſturb the order of the camp. He inſulted without neceſſity the religion of his Sovereign and of his country, by the epithets of contempt which he bestowed on the Roman Gods. "Deos "vestros ligneos et lapideos adorare contemno, "quæ sunt idola surda et muta." Nay more; at the head of the legion, and in the face of the standards, the Centurion Marcellus openly renounced his allegiance to the Emperors. "Ex "hoc militare IMPERATORIBUS VESTRIS de- "sisto." From this moment I no longer serve YOUR EMPERORS, are the important words of Marcellus, which his advocate has not thought proper to translate. I again make my appeal to any lawyer, to any military man, Whether, under such circumstances, the pronoun *your* has not a seditious, and even treasonable, import? And whether the officer who should make this declaration, and at the same time throw away his sword at the head of the regiment, would not be condemned for mutiny and desertion by any court-martial in Europe? I am the rather disposed to judge favourably of the conduct of the Roman government, as I cannot discover any desire to take advantage of the indiscretion of Marcellus. The Commander of the Legion seemed to lament that it was not in his power to dissemble this rash action. After a delay of more than three months, the Centurion was examined before the Vice-præfect, his superior Judge, who offered him the fairest opportunities of explaining or qualifying his seditious expressions, and at

last

laſt condemned him to loſe his head; not ſimply becauſe he was a Chriſtian, but becauſe he had violated his military oath, thrown away his belt, and publicly blaſphemed the Gods and the Emperors. Perhaps the impartial reader will confirm the ſentence of the Vice-Præfect Agricolanus, "Ita ſe habent facta "Marcelli, ut hæc *diſciplinâ* debeant vindi-"cari."

Notwithſtanding the plaineſt evidence, Dr. Chelſum will not believe that either Origen in Theory, or Marcellus in Practice, could ſeriouſly object to the uſe of arms; "becauſe it is "well known, that, far from declining the bu-"ſineſs of war altogether, whole legions of "Chriſtians ſerved in the Imperial armies[8]." I have not yet diſcovered, in the Author or Authors of the Remarks, many traces of a clear and enlightened underſtanding, yet I cannot ſuppoſe them ſo deſtitute of every reaſoning principle, as to imagine that they here allude to the conduct of the Chriſtians who embraced the profeſſion of arms after their religion had obtained a public eſtabliſhment. Whole legions of Chriſtians ſerved under the banners of Conſtantine and Juſtinian, as whole regiments of Chriſtians are now inliſted in the ſervice of France or England. The repreſentation which

[8] Chelſum, p. 113.

I had

I had given, was confined to the principles and practice of the Church of which Origen and Marcellus were members, before the ſenſe of public and private intereſt had reduced the lofty ſtandard of Evangelical perfection to the ordinary level of human nature. In thoſe primitive times, where are the Chriſtian legions that ſerved in the Imperial armies? Our Eccleſiaſtical Pompeys may ſtamp with their foot, but no armed men will ariſe out of the earth, except the ghoſts of the Thundering and the Thebæan legions; the former renowned for a Miracle, and the latter for a Martyrdom. Either the two Proteſtant Doctors muſt acquieſce under ſome imputations which are better underſtood than expreſſed, or they muſt prepare, in the full light and freedom of the eighteenth century, to undertake the defence of two obſolete legends, the leaſt abſurd of which ſtaggered the well-diſciplined credulity of a Franciſcan Friar. (See Pagi Critic. ad Annal. Baronii, A. D. 174. tom. i. p. 168.) Very different was the ſpirit and taſte of the learned and ingenuous Dr. Jortin, who, after treating the ſilly ſtory of the Thundering Legion with the contempt it deſerved, continues in the following words: " Moyle wiſhes no greater " penance to the believers of the Thundering " Legion, than that they may alſo believe " the Martyrdom of the Thebæan Legion.

" (Moyle's

" (Moyle's Works, vol. ii. p. 103): to which " good wiſh, I ſay with Le Clerc (Bibliotheque " A. et M. tom. xxvii. p. 193) AMEN.

" Qui Bavium non odit, amet tua carmina, Mævi."

(Jortin's Remarks on Eccleſiaſtical Hiſtory, vol. i. p. 367. 2d edition. London, 1767.)

Yet I ſhall not attempt to conceal a formidable army of Chriſtians and even of Martyrs, which is ready to inliſt under the banners of the confederate Doctors, if they will accept their ſervice. As a ſpecimen of the extravagant legends of the middle age, I had produced the inſtance of ten thouſand Chriſtian ſoldiers ſuppoſed to have been crucified on Mount Ararat, by the order either of Trajan or Hadrian [1]. For the mention and for the confutation of this ſtory, I had appealed to a Papiſt and a Proteſtant, to the learned Tillemont (Mem. Eccleſiaſt. tom. ii. part ii. p. 438), and to the diligent Geddes (Miſcellanies, vol. ii. p. 203), and when Tillemont was not afraid to ſay that there are few hiſtories which appear more fabulous, I was not aſhamed of diſmiſſing the *Fable* with ſilent contempt. We may trace the degrees of fiction as well as thoſe of credibility, and the impartial Critic will not place on the ſame level the baptiſm of Philip and the donation of Conſtantine. But in conſidering the crucifix-

[1] Gibbon, p. 654. Note 74.

ion

ion of the ten thousand Christian soldiers, we are not reduced to the necessity of weighing any internal probabilities, or of disproving any external testimonies. This legend, the absurdity of which must strike every *rational* mind, stands naked and unsupported by the authority of any writer who lived within a thousand years of the age of Trajan, and has not been able to obtain the poor sanction of the uncorrupted Martyrologies which were framed in the most credulous period of Ecclesiastical History. The two Protestant Doctors will probably reject the unsubstantial present which has been offered them; yet there is one of my adversaries, the *anonymous Gentleman*, who boldly declares himself the votary of the ten thousand Martyrs, and challenges me "to discredit a "FACT which hitherto by many has been "looked upon as well established [z]." It is pity that a prudent confessor did not whisper in his ear, that, although the martyrdom of these military Saints, like that of the eleven thousand Virgins, may contribute to the edification of the faithful, these wonderful tales should not be rashly exposed to the jealous and inquisitive eye of those profane Critics, whose examination always precedes, and sometimes checks, their Religious Assent.

[z] Remarks, p. 65, 66, 67.

II.

CHARACTER AND CREDIT OF EUSEBIUS.

A grave and pathetic complaint is introduced by Dr. Chelsum, into his preface [9], that Mr. Gibbon, who has often referred to the Fathers of the Church, seems to have entertained a general distrust of those respectable witnesses. The Critic is scandalized at the epithets of scanty and *suspicious*, which are applied to the materials of Ecclesiastical History; and if he cannot impeach the truth of the former, he censures in the most angry terms the injustice of the latter. He assumes, with peculiar zeal, the defence of Eusebius, the venerable parent of Ecclesiastical History, and labours to rescue his character from the *gross misrepresentation* on which Mr. Gibbon has openly insisted [1]. He observes, as if he sagaciously foresaw the objection, "That it will not be "sufficient here to allege a few instances of "apparent credulity in some of the Fathers, "in order to fix a general charge of *suspition* "on all." But it *may* be sufficient to allege a clear and fundamental principle of historical as well as legal Criticism, that whenever we are destitute of the means of comparing the testimonies of the opposite parties, the evidence of *any* witness, however illustrious by his rank

[9] P. ii, iii.

[1] Chelsum and Randolph, p. 210—238.

and

and titles, is justly to be *suspected* in his own cause. It is unfortunate enough, that I should be engaged with adversaries, whom their habits of study and conversation appear to have left in total ignorance of the principles which universally regulate the opinions and practice of mankind.

As the ancient world was not distracted by the fierce conflicts of hostile sects, the free and eloquent writers of Greece and Rome had few opportunities of indulging their passions, or of exercising their impartiality in the relation of religious events. Since the origin of Theological Factions, some Historians, Ammianus Marcellinus, Fra-Paolo, Thuanus, Hume, and perhaps a few others, have deserved the singular praise of holding the balance with a steady and equal hand. Independent and unconnected, they contemplated with the same indifference, the opinions and interests of the contending parties; or, if they were seriously attached to a particular system, they were armed with a firm and moderate temper, which enabled them to suppress their affections, and to sacrifice their resentments. In this small, but *venerable* Synod of Historians, Eusebius cannot claim a seat. I had aknowledged, and I still think, that his character was less tinctured with credulity than that of most of his contemporaries; but as his

enemies

enemies must admit, that he was sincere and earnest in the profession of Christianity, so the warmest of his admirers, or at least of his readers, must discern, and will probably applaud, the religious zeal which disgraces or adorns every page of his Ecclesiastical History. This laborious and useful work was published at a time, between the defeat of Licinius and the Council of Nice, when the resentment of the Christians was still warm, and when the Pagans were astonished and dismayed by the recent victory and conversion of the great Constantine. The materials, I shall dare to repeat the invidious epithets of scanty and suspicious, were extracted from the accounts which the Christians themselves had given of their *own* sufferings, and of the cruelty of their enemies. The Pagans had so long and so contemptuously neglected the rising greatness of the Church, that the Bishop of Cæsarea had little either to hope or to fear from the writers of the opposite party; almost all of that *little* which did exist, has been accidentally lost, or purposely destroyed; and the candid enquirer may vainly wish to compare with the History of Eusebius, some Heathen narrative of the persecutions of Decius and Diocletian. Under these circumstances, it is the duty of an impartial judge to be counsel for the prisoner, who is incapable of making any defence for himself; and it is the

first

first office of a counsel to examine with distrust and *suspicion*, the interested evidence of the accuser. Reason justifies the suspicion, and it is confirmed by the constant experience of modern History, in almost every instance where we have an opportunity of comparing the mutual complaints and apologies of the religious factions, who have disturbed each other's happiness in this world, for the sake of securing it in the next.

As we are deprived of the means of contrasting the adverse relations of the Christians and Pagans; it is the more incumbent on us to improve the opportunities of trying the narratives of Eusebius, by the original, and sometimes occasional, testimonies of the more ancient writers of his own party. Dr. Chelsum[a] has observed, that the celebrated passage of Origen, which has so much thinned the ranks of the army of Martyrs, must be confined to the persecutions that had already happened. I cannot dispute this sagacious remark, but I shall venture to add, that this passage more immediately relates to the religious tempests which had been excited in the time and country of Origen; and still more particularly to the city of Alexandria, and to the persecution of Severus, in which young Origen successfully exhorted his father, to sacrifice his life and

[a] Gibbon, p. 653. Chelsum, p. 204—207.

fortune

fortune for the cause of Christ. From such unquestionable evidence, I am authorised to conclude, that the number of holy victims who sealed their faith with their blood, was not, on this occasion, very considerable: but I cannot reconcile this fair conclusion with the positive declaration of Eusebius (l. vi. c. 2. p. 258), that at Alexandria, in the persecution of Severus, an innumerable, at least an indefinite multitude (μυριοι) of Christians were honoured with the crown of Martyrdom. The advocates for Eusebius may exert their critical skill in proving that μυριοι and ολιγοι *many* and *few*, are synonymous and convertible terms, but they will hardly succeed in diminishing so palpable a contradiction, or in removing the suspicion which deeply fixes itself on the historical character of the Bishop of Cæsarea. This unfortunate experiment taught me to read, with becoming caution, the loose and declamatory style which *seems* to magnify the multitude of Martyrs and Confessors, and to aggravate the nature of their sufferings. From the same motives I selected, with careful observation, the more certain account of the number of persons who actually suffered death in the province of Palestine, during the whole eight years of the last and most rigorous persecution.

Besides the reasonable grounds of suspicion, which suggest themselves to every liberal mind, against the credibility of the Ecclesiastical Historians, and of Eusebius, their venerable leader, I had taken notice of two very remarkable passages of the Bishop of Cæsarea. He frankly, or at least indirectly, declares, that in treating of the last persecution, "he has related whatever might redound to the glory, "and suppressed all that could tend to the "disgrace, of Religion [3]." Dr. Chelsum, who, on this occasion, most lamentably exclaims that we should hear Eusebius, before we utterly condemn him, has provided, with the assistance of his worthy colleague, an elaborate defence for their common patron; and as if he were secretly conscious of the weakness of the cause, he has contrived the resource of intrenching himself in a very muddy soil, behind three several fortifications, which do not exactly support each other. The advocate for the sincerity of Eusebius maintains: 1st, That he never made such a declaration: 2dly, That he had a right to make it: and, 3dly, That he did not observe it. These separate and almost inconsistent apologies, I shall separately consider.

1. Dr. Chelsum is at a loss how to reconcile,——I beg pardon for weakening the force of his dogmatic style; he declares, that "It is "plainly impossible to reconcile the express

[3] Gibbon, p. 699.

"words of the charge exhibited, with any "part of either of the passages appealed to in "support of it[4]." If he means, as I think he must, that the *express words* of my text cannot be found in that of Eusebius, I congratulate the importance of the discovery. But was it possible? Could it be my design to quote the words of Eusebius, when I reduced into one sentence the spirit and substance of two diffuse and distinct passages? If I have given the true sense and meaning of the Ecclesiastical Historian, I have discharged the duties of a fair Interpreter; nor shall I refuse to rest the proof of my fidelity on the translation of those two passages of Eusebius, which Dr. Chelsum produces in his favour[5]. "But it is not our "part to describe the sad calamities which at "last befel them (the *Christians*), since it does "not agree with our plan to relate their dissentions and wickedness before the persecu-"tion; on which account we have determined "to relate nothing more concerning them than "may serve to justify the Divine Judgment. "We therefore have not been induced to "make mention either of those who were "tempted in the persecution, or of those who "made utter shipwreck of their salvation, and "who were sunk of their own accord in the

[4] Chelsum, p. 232. [5] P. 228. 231.

"depths

" depths of the ſtorm; but ſhall only add " thoſe things to our General Hiſtory, which " may in the firſt place be profitable to our- " ſelves, and afterwards to poſterity." In the other paſſage, Euſebius, after mentioning the diſſentions of the Confeſſors among themſelves, again declares that it is his intention to paſs over all theſe things. " Whatſoever things, " (continues the Hiſtorian, in the words of " the Apoſtle, who was recommending the " practice of virtue) whatſoever things are " honeſt, whatſoever things are of good re- " port, if there be any virtue, and if there be " any praiſe; theſe things Euſebius thinks " moſt ſuitable to a Hiſtory of Martyrs;" of *wonderful* Martyrs, is the ſplendid epithet which Dr. Chelſum had not thought proper to tranſ- late. I ſhould betray a very mean opinion of the judgment and candour of my readers, if I added a ſingle reflection on the clear and ob- vious tendency of the two paſſages of the Ec- cleſiaſtical Hiſtorian. I ſhall only obſerve, that the Biſhop of Cæſarea ſeems to have claim- ed a privilege of a ſtill more dangerous and extenſive nature. In one of the moſt learned and elaborate works that antiquity has left us, the Thirty-ſecond Chapter of the Twelfth Book of his Evangelical Preparation bears for its title this ſcandalous Propoſition, " How it may be " lawful and fitting to uſe falſehood as a me-

 " dicine,

"dicine, and for the benefit of those who want "to be deceived." Οτι δεησει ποτε τῳ ψευδει αντι φαρμακου χρησθαι επι ωφελειᾳ των δεομενων τε τοιουτου τροπου. (P. 356, Edit. Græc. Rob. Stephani, Paris 1544.) In this chapter he alleges a passage of Plato, which approves the occasional practice of pious and salutary frauds; nor is Eusebius ashamed to justify the sentiments of the Athenian philosopher by the example of the sacred writers of the Old Testament.

2. I had contented myself with observing, that Eusebius had violated one of the fundamental laws of history, *Ne quid veri dicere non audeat*; nor could I imagine, if the *fact* was allowed, that any question could possibly arise upon the matter of *right*. I was indeed mistaken; and I now begin to understand why I have given so little satisfaction to Dr. Chelsum, and to other critics of the same complexion, as our ideas of the duties and the privileges of an historian appear to be so widely different. It is alleged, that "every writer has a right to "chuse his subject, for the particular benefit "of his reader; that he has explained his own "plan consistently; that he considers himself, "according to it, not as a complete historian "of the times, but rather as a *didactic* writer, "whose main object is to make his work, like "the Scriptures themselves, PROFITABLE FOR "DOCTRINE;

"DOCTRINE; that, as he treats only of the af-" fairs of the Church, the plan is at least ex-" cusable, perhaps peculiarly proper; and that" he has conformed himself to the principal" duty of an historian, while, according to his" immediate design, he has not particularly" related any of the transactions which could" tend to the disgrace of religion [6]." The historian must indeed be generous, who will conceal, by his own disgrace, that of his country, or of his religion. Whatever subject he has chosen, whatever persons he introduces, he owes to himself, to the present age, and to posterity, a just and perfect delineation of all that may be praised, of all that may be excused, and of all that must be censured. If he fails in the discharge of his important office, he partially violates the sacred obligations of truth, and disappoints his readers of the instruction which they might have derived from a fair parallel of the vices and virtues of the most illustrious characters. Herodotus might range without controul in the spacious walks of the Greek and Barbaric domain, and Thucydides might confine his steps to the narrow path of the Peloponnesian war; but those historians would never have deserved the esteem of posterity, if they had designedly suppressed or tran-

[6] Chelsum, p. 229, 230, 231.

fiently mentioned thofe facts which could tend to the difgrace of Greece or of Athens. Thefe unalterable dictates of confcience and reafon have been *feldom* queftioned, though they have been feldom obferved; and we muft fincerely join in the honeft complaint of Melchior Canus, "that the lives of the philofophers have "been compofed by Laertius, and thofe of "the Cæfars by Suetonius, with a much "ftricter and more fevere regard for hiftoric "truth, than can be found in the lives of "faints and martyrs, as they are defcribed by "Catholic writers." (See Loci Communes, l. xi. p. 650, apud Clericum, Epiftol. Critic. v. p. 136.) And yet the partial reprefentation of truth is of far more pernicious confequence in ecclefiaftical, than in civil, hiftory. If Laertius had concealed the defects of Plato, or if Suetonius had difguifed the vices of Auguftus, we fhould have been deprived of the knowledge of fome curious, and perhaps inftructive, facts, and our idea of thofe celebrated men might have been more favourable than they deferved; but I cannot difcover any practical inconveniencies which could have been the refult of our ignorance. But if Eufebius had fairly and circumftantially related the fcandalous diffentions of the Confeffors; if he had fhewn that their virtues were tinctured with pride and obftinacy, and that their lively faith was not exempt from some mixture of enthusiasm; he would have armed his readers against the excessive veneration for those holy men, which imperceptibly degenerated into religious worship. The success of these *didactic* histories, by concealing or palliating every circumstance of human infirmity, was one of the most efficacious means of consecrating the memory, the bones, and the writings of the saints of the prevailing party; and a great part of the errors and corruptions of the Church of Rome may fairly be ascribed to this criminal dissimulation of the ecclesiastical historians. As a Protestant Divine, Dr. Chelsum must abhor these corruptions; but as a Christian, he should be careful lest his apology for the prudent choice of Eusebius should fix an indirect censure on the unreserved sincerity of the four Evangelists. Instead of confining their narrative to those things which are virtuous and of good report, instead of following the plan which is here recommended as *peculiarly proper* for the affairs of the Church, the inspired writers have thought it their duty to relate the most minute circumstances of the fall of St. Peter, without considering whether the behaviour of an Apostle, who thrice denied his Divine Master, might redound to the honour, or to the disgrace, of Christianity. If Dr. Chelsum should be frightened by this unexpected consequence, if he should be desirous

of

of saving his faith from *utter shipwreck*, by throwing over-board the useless lumber of memory and reflection, I am not enough his enemy to impede the success of his honest endeavours.

The didactic method of writing history was still more profitably exercised by Eusebius in another work, which he has intitled, The Life of Constantine, his gracious patron and benefactor. Priests and poets have enjoyed in every age a privilege of flattery; but if the actions of Constantine are compared with the perfect idea of a royal saint, which, under his name, has been delineated by the zeal and gratitude of Eusebius, the most indulgent reader will confess, that when I styled him a *courtly Bishop* [7], I could only be restrained by my respect for the episcopal character from the use of a much harsher epithet. The other appellation of a *passionate declaimer*, which seems to have sounded still more offensive in the tender ears of Dr. Chelsum [8], was not applied by me to Eusebius, but to Lactantius, or rather to the author of the historical declamation, *De mortibus persecutorum*; and indeed it is much more properly adapted to the Rhetorician, than to the Bishop. Each of those authors was alike studious of the glory of Constantine; but each

[7] Gibbon, p. 704. [8] Chelsum, p. 234.

of

of them directed the torrent of his invectives against the tyrant, whether Maxentius or Licinius, whose recent defeat was the actual theme of popular and Christian applause. This simple observation may serve to extinguish a very trifling objection of my critic, That Eusebius has not represented the tyrant Maxentius under the character of a Persecutor.

Without scrutinizing the considerations of interest which might support the integrity of Baronius and Tillemont, I may fairly observe, that both those learned Catholics have acknowledged and condemned the dissimulation of Eusebius, which is partly denied, and partly justified, by my adversary. The honourable reflection of Baronius well deserves to be transcribed. "Hæc (the passages already quoted) "de suo in conscribendâ persecutionis historia "Eusebius; parum explens numeros sui mu-"neris; dum perinde ac si panegyrim scribe-"ret non historiam, triumphos dumtaxat mar-"tyrum atque victorias, non autem lapsus "jacturamque fidelium posteris scripturæ mo-"numentis curaret." (Baron. Annal. Eccle-siast. A. D. 302, N° 11. See likewise Tillemont, Mem. Eccles. tom. v. p. 62, 156; tom. vii. p. 130.) In a former instance, Dr. Chelsum appeared to be more credulous than a Monk: on the present occasion, he has shewn

himself

himself less sincere than a Cardinal, and more obstinate than a Jansenist.

3. Yet the advocate for Eusebius has still another expedient in reserve. Perhaps he made the unfortunate declaration of his partial design, perhaps he had a right to make it; but at least his accuser must admit, that he has saved his honour by not keeping his word; since I myself have taken notice of THE CORRUPTION OF MANNERS AND PRINCIPLES among the Christians, so FORCIBLY LAMENTED by Eusebius[9]. He has indeed indulged himself in a strain of *loose* and *indefinite* censure, which may generally be just, and which cannot be personally offensive, which is alike incapable of wounding or of correcting, as it seems to have no fixed object or certain aim. Juvenal might have read his satire against women in a circle of Roman ladies, and each of them might have listened with pleasure to the amusing description of the various vices and follies, from which she herself was so perfectly free. The moralist, the preacher, the ecclesiastical historian, enjoy a still more ample latitude of invective; and as long as they abstain from any particular censure, they may securely expose, and even exaggerate, the sins of the multitude. The precepts of Christianity seem to inculcate

[9] Chelsum, p. 226, 227.

a style

a style of mortification, of abasement, of self-contempt; and the hypocrite who aspires to the reputation of a saint, often finds it convenient to affect the language of a penitent. I should doubt whether Dr. Chelsum is much acquainted with the comedies of Moliere. If he has ever read that inimitable master of human life, he may recollect whether Tartuffe was very much inclined to confess his real guilt, when he exclaimed,

> Oui, mon Frere, je suis un mechant, un coupable;
> Un malheureux pécheur, tout plein d'iniquité;
> Le plus grand scelerat qui ait jamais été.
> Chaque instant de ma vie est chargé de souillures,
> Elle n'est qu'un amas de crimes et d'ordures.
> . . . .
> Oui, mon cher fils, parlez, traitez moi de perfide,
> D'infame, de perdu, de voleur, d'homicide;
> Accablez moi de noms encore plus detestés:
> Je n'y contredis point, je les ai merités,
> Et j'en veux à genoux souffrir l'ignominie,
> Comme une honte due aux crimes de ma vie.

It is not my intention to compare the character of Tartuffe with that of Eusebius; the former pointed his invectives against himself, the latter directed them against the times in which he had lived: but as the prudent Bishop of Cæsarea did not specify any place or person for the object of his censure, he cannot justly be accused, even by his friends, of violating the *profitable* plan of his *didactic* history.

The extreme caution of Eusebius, who declines any mention of those who were tempted and who fell during the persecution, has countenanced a suspicion that he himself was one of those unhappy victims, and that his tenderness for the wounded fame of his brethren arose from a just apprehension of his own disgrace. In one of my notes[1], I had observed, that he was charged with the guilt of some criminal compliances, in his own presence, and in the Council of Tyre. I am therefore accountable for the reality only, and not for the truth, of the accusation: but as the two Doctors, who on this occasion unite their forces, are angry and clamorous in asserting the innocence of the Ecclesiastical Historian[2], I shall advance one step farther, and shall maintain, that the charge against Eusebius, though not legally proved, is supported by a reasonable share of presumptive evidence.

I have often wondered why our orthodox Divines should be so earnest and zealous in the defence of Eusebius; whose moral character cannot be preserved, unless by the sacrifice of a more illustrious, and, as I really believe, of a more innocent victim. Either the Bishop of Cæsarea, on a very important occasion, vio-

[1] Gibbon, p. 699, N. 178.
[2] Chelsum and Randolph, p. 236, 237, 238.

lated the laws of Chriſtian charity and civil juſtice, or we muſt fix a charge of calumny, almoſt of forgery, on the head of the great Athanaſius, the ſtandard-bearer of the Homoouſian cauſe, and the firmeſt pillar of the Catholic faith. In the Council of Tyre, he was accuſed of murdering, or at leaſt of mutilating, a Biſhop, whom he produced at Tyre alive and unhurt (Athanaſ. tom. i. p. 783. 786.); and of ſacrilegiouſly breaking a conſecrated chalice, in a village where neither church, nor altar, nor chalice, could poſſibly have exiſted. (Athanaſ. tom. i. p. 731, 732. 802.) Notwithſtanding the cleareſt proofs of his innocence, Athanaſius was oppreſſed by the Arian faction; and Euſebius of Cæſarea, the venerable father of Eccleſiaſtical hiſtory, conducted this iniquitous proſecution from a motive of perſonal enmity. (Athanaſ. tom. i. p. 728. 795. 797.) Four years afterwards, a national council of the Biſhops of Egypt, forty-nine of whom had been preſent at the Synod of Tyre, addreſſed an epiſtle or manifeſto in favour of Athanaſius to all the Biſhops of the Chriſtian world. In this epiſtle they aſſert, that ſome of the Confeſſors, who accompanied them to Tyre, had accuſed Euſebius of Cæſarea of an act relative to idolatrous ſacrifice. ϰϰ Ευσεϐιος ὁ εν Καισερεια της Παλαιστινης επι θυσια κατηγορειτο ὑπο των συν ἡμιν ὁμολογητων. (Athanaſ.

naſ. tom. i. p. 728.) Beſides this ſhort and authentic memorial, which eſcaped the knowledge or the candour of our confederate Doctors, a conſonant but more circumſtantial narrative of the accuſation of Euſebius may be found in the writings of Epiphanius (Hæreſ. lxviii. p. 723, 724.), the learned Biſhop of Salamis, who was born about the time of the Synod of Tyre. He relates, that, in one of the ſeſſions of the Council, Potamon, Biſhop of Heraclea in Egypt, addreſſed Euſebius in the following words: "How now, Euſebius, can "this be borne, that you ſhould be ſeated as "a judge, while the innocent Athanaſius "is left ſtanding as a criminal? Tell me, "continued Potamon, were we not in priſon "together during the perſecution? For my "own part, I loſt an eye for the ſake of the "truth; but I cannot diſcern that *you* have "loſt any one of your members. You bear "not any marks of your ſufferings for Jeſus "Chriſt; but here you are, full of life, and "with all the parts of your body ſound and "entire! How could you contrive to eſcape "from priſon, unleſs you ſtained your conſcience, either by actual guilt or by a criminal promiſe to our perſecutors?" Euſebius immediately broke up the meeting, and diſcovered by his anger, that he was confound-

ed

ed or provoked by the reproaches of the Confessor Potamon.

I should despise myself, if I were capable of magnifying, for a present occasion, the authority of the witness whom I have produced. Potamon was most assuredly actuated by a strong prejudice against the personal enemy of his Primate; and if the transaction to which he alluded had been of a private and doubtful kind, I would not take any ungenerous advantage of the respect which my Reverend Adversaries must entertain for the character of a Confessor. But I cannot distrust the veracity of Potamon, when he confined himself to the assertion of a fact, which lay within the compass of his personal knowledge: and collateral testimony (See Photius, p. 296, 297.) attests, that Eusebius was long enough in prison to assist his friend, the Martyr Pamphilus, in composing the first five books of his Apology for Origen. If we admit that Eusebius was imprisoned, he must have been discharged, and his discharge must have been either honourable, or criminal, or innocent. If his patience vanquished the cruelty of the Tyrant's Ministers, a short relation of his own confession and sufferings would have formed an useful and edifying Chapter in his Didactic History of the Persecution of Palestine; and the Reader would have been satisfied of the veracity of an Historian who valued truth above

his

his life. If it had been in his power to juſtify, or even to excuſe, the manner of his diſcharge from priſon, it was his intereſt, it was his duty, to prevent the doubts and ſuſpicions which muſt ariſe from his ſilence under theſe delicate circumſtances. Notwithſtanding theſe urgent reaſons, Euſebius has obſerved a profound, and perhaps a prudent, ſilence: though he frequently celebrates the merit and martyrdom of his friend Pamphilus (p. 371. 394. 419. 427. Edit. Cantab.), he never inſinuates that he was his companion in priſon; and while he copiouſly deſcribes the eight years perſecution in Paleſtine, he never repreſents himſelf in any other light than that of a ſpectator. Such a conduct in a Writer, who relates with a viſible ſatisfaction the honourable events of his own life, if it be not abſolutely conſidered as an evidence of conſcious guilt, muſt excite, and may juſtify, the ſuſpicions of the moſt candid Critic.

Yet the firmneſs of Dr. Randolph is not ſhaken by theſe rational ſuſpicions; and he condeſcends, in a magiſterial tone, to inform me, "That it is highly improbable, from the "general well-known deciſion of the Church "in ſuch caſes, that had his apoſtacy been "known, he would have riſen to thoſe high "honours which he attained, or been admitted "at all indeed to any other than lay-com-"munion." This weighty objection did not ſurpriſe

surprise me, as I had already seen the substance of it in the Prolegomena of Valesius; but I safely disregarded a difficulty which had not appeared of any moment to the national council of Egypt; and I still think that an hundred Bishops, with Athanasius at their head, were as competent judges of the discipline of the fourth Century, as even the Lady Margaret's Professor of Divinity in the University of Oxford. As a work of supererogation, I have consulted, however, the Antiquities of Bingham (See l. iv. c. 3. s. 6, 7. vol. i. p. 144, &c. fol. edit.), and found, as I expected, that much real learning had made him cautious and modest. After a careful examination of the facts and authorities already known to me, and of those with which I was supplied by the diligent Antiquarian, I am persuaded that the theory and the practice of discipline were not invariably the same, that particular examples cannot always be reconciled with general rules, and that the stern laws of justice often yielded to motives of policy and convenience. The temper of Jerom towards those whom he considered as Heretics, was fierce and unforgiving; yet the Dialogue of Jerom against the Luciferians, which I have read with infinite pleasure (tom. ii. p. 135—147. Edit. Basil. 1536.), is the seasonable and dextrous performance of a Statesman, who felt the expediency

diency of ſoothing and reconciling a numerous party of offenders. The moſt rigid diſcipline, with regard to the Eccleſiaſtics who had fallen in time of perſecution, is expreſſed in the 10th Canon of the Council of Nice; the moſt remarkable indulgence was ſhewn by the Fathers of the ſame Council to the *lapſed*, the degraded, the ſchiſmatic Biſhop of Lycopolis. Of the penitent ſinners, ſome might eſcape the ſhame of a public conviction or confeſſion, and others might be exempted from the rigour of clerical puniſhment. If Euſebius incurred the guilt of a ſacrilegious promiſe (for we are free to accept the milder alternative of Potamon), the proofs of this criminal tranſaction might be ſuppreſſed by the influence of money or favour; a ſeaſonable journey into Egypt might allow time for the popular rumours to ſubſide. The crime of Euſebius might be protected by the impunity of many Epiſcopal Apoſtates (See Philoſtorg. l. ii. c. 15. p. 21. Edit. Gothofred.); and the Governors of the Church very reaſonably deſired to retain in their ſervice the moſt learned Chriſtian of the Age.

Before I return theſe ſheets to the preſs, I muſt not forget an anonymous pamphlet, which, under the title of *A Few Remarks*, &c. was publiſhed againſt my Hiſtory in the courſe of the laſt ſummer. The unknown writer has thought proper

to

to distinguish himself by the emphatic, yet vague, appellation of A Gentleman: but I must lament that he has not considered, with becoming attention, the duties of that respectable character. I am ignorant of the motives which can urge a man of a liberal mind, and liberal manners, to attack without provocation, and without tenderness, any work which may have contributed to the information, or even to the amusement, of the Public. But I am well convinced, that the author of such a work, who boldly gives his name and his labours to the world, imposes on his adversaries the fair and honourable obligation of encountering him in open day-light, and of supporting the weight of their assertions by the credit of their names. The effusions of wit, or the productions of reason, may be accepted from a secret and unknown hand. The critic who attempts to injure the reputation of another, by strong imputations which may possibly be false, should renounce the ungenerous hope of concealing behind a mask the vexation of disappointment, and the guilty blush of detection.

After this remark, which I cannot make without some degree of concern, I shall frankly declare, that it is not my wish or my intention to prosecute with this *Gentleman* a literary altercation. There lies between us a broad and unfathomable gulph; and the heavy mist of prejudice and superstition, which has in a great measure been dispelled by the free inquiries of the present age, still continues to involve the mind of my Adversary. He fondly embraces those phantoms (for instance, an imaginary Pilate [1]), which can scarcely find a shelter in the gloom of an Italian convent; and the resentment which he points against me, might frequently be extended to the most enlightened of the PROTESTANT, or, in his opinion, of the HERETICAL critics. His observations are divided into a number of unconnected paragraphs, each of which contains some quotation from my History, and the angry, yet commonly trifling, expression of his disapprobation and displeasure. Those sentiments I cannot hope to remove; and as the religious opinions of this *Gentleman* are principally founded on the infallibility of the Church [2], they are not calculated to make a very deep impression on the mind of an English reader. The view of *facts* will be materially affected by the contagious influence of *doctrines*. The man who refuses to judge of the conduct of Lewis XIV. and Charles V. towards their Protestant subjects [3], declares himself incapable of distinguishing the limits of persecution and toleration. The devout Papist, who has implored

[1] Remarks, p. 100. [2] Id. p. 15. [3] Id. p. 111.

on his knees the interceſſion of St. Cyprian, will ſeldom preſume to examine the actions of the Saint by the rules of hiſtorical evidence and of moral propriety. Inſtead of the homely likeneſs which I had exhibited of the Biſhop of Carthage, my Adverſary has ſubſtituted a life of Cyprian [4], full of what the French call *onction*, and the Engliſh, *canting* (See Jortin's Remarks, Vol. ii. p. 239.): to which I can only reply, that thoſe who are diſſatisfied with the principles of Moſheim and Le Clerc, *muſt* view with eyes very different from mine, the Eccleſiaſtical Hiſtory of the third century.

It would be an *endleſs* diſcuſſion (*endleſs* in every ſenſe of the word), were I to examine the cavils which ſtart up and expire in every page of this criticiſm, on the inexhauſtible topic of opinions, characters, and intentions. Moſt of the inſtances which are here produced, are of ſo brittle a ſubſtance that they fall in pieces as ſoon as they are touched: and I ſearched for ſome time before I was able to diſcover an example of ſome moment where the *Gentleman* had fairly ſtaked his veracity againſt ſome poſitive fact aſſerted in the Two laſt Chapters of my Hiſtory. At laſt I perceived that he has abſolutely denied [5] that any thing can be gathered from the Epiſtles of St. Cyprian, or from

[4] Remarks, p. 72—88. [5] Id. p. 90, 91.

 his

his treatiſe *De Unitate Eccleſiæ*, to which I had referred, to juſtify my account of the ſpiritual pride and licentious manners of ſome of the Confeſſors [6]. As the *numbers* of the Epiſtles are not the ſame in the edition of Pamelius and in that of Fell, the Critic may be excuſed for miſtaking my quotations, if he will acknowledge that he was ignorant of eccleſiaſtical hiſtory, and that he never heard of the troubles excited by the ſpiritual pride of the Confeſſors, who uſurped the privilege of giving letters of communion to penitent ſinners. But my reference to the treatiſe *De Unitate Eccleſiæ* was clear and direct; the treatiſe itſelf contains only ten pages, and the following words might be diſtinctly read by any perſon who underſtood the Latin language. "Nec quiſquam "miretur, dilectiſſimi fratres, etiam de confeſſo-"ribus quoſdam ad iſta procedere, inde quoque "aliquos tam nefanda tam gravia peccare. Ne-"que enim confeſſio immunem facit ab inſidiis "diaboli; aut contra tentationes, et pericula, et "incurſus atque impetus ſeculares adhuc in ſe-"culo poſitum perpetuâ ſecuritate defendit: ce-"terum nunquam in confeſſoribus, *fraudes*, et "*ſtupra*, et *adulteria* poſtmodum videremus, quæ "nunc in quibuſdam videntes ingemiſcimus et "dolemus." This formal declaration of Cyprian,

[6] Gibbon, p. 661, Note 91.

which is followed by ſeveral long periods of admonition and cenſure, is alone ſufficient to expoſe the ſcandalous vices of ſome of the Confeſſors, and the diſingenuous behaviour of my concealed adverſary.

After this example, which I have fairly choſen as one of the moſt ſpecious and important of his objections, the candid Reader would excuſe me, if from this moment I declined *the Gentleman*'s acquaintance. But as two topics have occurred, which are intimately connected with the ſubject of the preceding ſheets, I have inſerted each of them in its proper place, as the concluſion of the fourth article of my anſwers to Mr. Davis, and of the firſt article of my reply to the confederate Doctors, Chelſum and Randolph.

It is not without ſome mixture of mortification and regret, that I now look back on the number of hours which I have conſumed, and the number of pages which I have filled, in vindicating my literary and moral character from the charge of wilful *Miſrepreſentations*, groſs *Errors*, and ſervile *Plagiariſms*. I cannot derive any triumph or conſolation from the occaſional advantages which I may have gained over three adverſaries, whom it is impoſſible for me to conſider as objects either of terror or of eſteem. The ſpirit of reſentment, and every

every other lively ſenſation, have long ſince been extinguiſhed; and the pen would long ſince have dropped from my weary hand, had I not been ſupported in the execution of this ungrateful taſk, by the conſciouſneſs, or at leaſt by the opinion, that I was diſcharging a debt of honour to the Public and to myſelf. I am impatient to diſmiſs, and to diſmiſs FOR EVER, this odious controverſy, with the ſucceſs of which I cannot ſurely be elated; and I have only to requeſt, that, as ſoon as my Readers are convinced of my innocence, they would forget my Vindication.

Bentinck-Street,
February 3. 1779.

FINIS.

N. B. If any ſlips of the pen, or errors of the preſs, ſhould ſtill remain in this *ſecond* Edition, I muſt make my appeal, not to the candour of my Adverſaries, but to the indulgence of the Public.

www.ingramcontent.com/pod-product-compliance
Lightning Source LLC
Chambersburg PA
CBHW020553270326
41927CB00006B/824